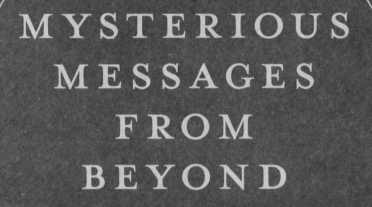

MYSTERIOUS
MESSAGES
FROM
BEYOND

VON BRASCHLER

REDFeather™
MIND | BODY | SPIRIT

4880 Lower Valley Road, Atglen, PA 19310

Other Schiffer Books by the Author:
Manifesting: Using Thought Forms to Visualize Real Change, ISBN 978-0-7643-6171-5

Other Schiffer Books on Related Subjects:
Disembodied Voices: True Accounts of Hidden Beings, Tim Marczenko, ISBN 978-0-7643-6023-7
Behind the Paranormal: Everything You Know Is Wrong, Paul Eno & Ben Eno, ISBN 978-0-7643-5222-5
Dancing Past the Graveyard: Poltergeists, Parasites, Parallel Worlds, and God, Paul Eno, ISBN 978-0-7643-5774-9

Cover design by Ashley Millhouse
Type set in Mrs. Eaves

ISBN: 978-0-7643-6286-6
Printed in India

Published by REDFeather Mind, Body, Spirit
An imprint of Schiffer Publishing, Ltd.
4880 Lower Valley Road
Atglen, PA 19310
Phone: (610) 593-1777; Fax: (610) 593-2002
Email: Info@schifferbooks.com
Web: www.redfeathermbs.com

For our complete selection of fine books on this and related subjects, please visit our website at www.schifferbooks.com. You may also write for a free catalog.

Schiffer Publishing's titles are available at special discounts for bulk purchases for sales promotions or premiums. Special editions, including personalized covers, corporate imprints, and excerpts, can be created in large quantities for special needs. For more information, contact the publisher.

We are always looking for people to write books on new and related subjects. If you have an idea for a book, please contact us at proposals@schifferbooks.com.

TABLE OF CONTENTS

FOREWORD

During the thirty years we have known each other, I personally witnessed the probing depths of Von Braschler's original insights into the unknown, real-life enigmas brought back into the light by his reader-friendly flair for describing them with penetrating, even dramatic, clarity. As such, his thoughts harmonize with our own, lingering in the mind and stirring within it new possibilities and perspectives long after the last page of any one of his books has been turned. *Mysterious Messages from Beyond: Learning to Listen* seems to me the finest distillation of everything that is best and brightest in this brilliant writer's considerable output.

It is especially dear to me, because I share with him a kindred passion for understanding the nature of metaphysical communication, as expressed in some of my own work, especially *Synchronicity and You* (Boston: Element Books, 1999), *Synchronicity as Mystical Experience* (Pine Mountain Club, CA: Shanti, 2017), and *Our Dolphin Ancestors* (Rochester VT: Bear, 2016). In these titles, I also explored paranormal potentials that more-conventional investigators dismiss out of hand as either naïve misinterpretations of quite ordinary and rationally inexplicable events or else self-delusional fantasy. Well, perception is impossible without at least a willingness to perceive. Sir Isaac Newton, if resurrected into the twentieth century and told that there are many millions of inaudible voices surrounding him at any one time, would either refuse to credit such nonsense or imagine himself in the presence of spiritualists—until someone turned on a radio.

So, too, *Mysterious Messages from Beyond* shows that otherworldly voices are no less part of our surroundings. We lack only the proper means to hear them, not some scientific device like a radio, although future developments in the improving technology of so-called spirit boxes may yet culminate in some kind of transcendental telephone. Until then, Von Braschler demonstrates that we need not wait for the future availability of such materialist means but may currently access all numinous audio waves infusing the environment with our inherited, built-in capacity for reception and transmission. We still possess this virtually lost, severely diminished talent from its inception 2.8 million years ago, when our earliest known ancestor made his first tool.

It is important in this regard to understand that *Homo habilis* and all his evolutionary descendants throughout subsequent generations depended for their second-to-second survival upon each individual's awareness of deadly threats constantly posed by the natural environment, from diligent predators to geological and ecological hazards. Against these ever-present, life-threatening challenges, the fundamental, vital prerequisite for early human existence absolutely depended on keen awareness of every nuance within striking distance. It was chiefly this developing sensitivity to perception that distinguished our forebears from other hominids less keenly cognizant of incessant, impending threats. These and other similarly slower anthropomorphic groups and their kind perished utterly and were forever left behind at an evolutionary dead end by that more alert tribe able to avoid or overcome obstacles more quickly foreseen, thanks to their better perception. You and I are the direct descendants of these psychic survivors. If so, what became of our instinctual legacy from them? The answer: civilization. The moment we forsook living in nature, our multimillion-year-old evolution of heightened perception and communication commenced to atrophy. Floors, walls, and ceilings physically cut off from the outside world. This process of alienation from our psychic roots accelerated and became more corrosive when houses clustered into hamlets for mutual protection, grew further into villages on behalf of bolstered security, morphed into towns and then cities through the demographic compulsion of overpopulation, and ultimately culminated in amorphic empires of insatiable greed and cultural paranoia, wherein ancestral powers were cynically relegated to fable and superstition. We are today where Rome, Babylon, Persia, Egypt, and many others—so alarmingly like ourselves and similarly certain of their guaranteed longevity—stood and fell before us at the close of the same, predictable cycle of self-destruction.

This new book is among the best of the last-ditch efforts by modern, alternative thinkers to direct us away from that lethal, historical pattern by seeking within ourselves for our lost heritage, still intact but buried under generational levels of disbelief. In my own three-decades-long research into synchronicity, I found that the phenomenon is sometimes a form of metaphysical communication, particularly through animals—not surprisingly, given their archetypical connections to human symbolism, but especially because they stand so much closer to nature than modern humans. They are, as my wife, Laura, defines them, "walkers between worlds." Accordingly, they make for wonderfully mysterious messengers—from lowly insects to Man's Best Friend—as the following examples demonstrate.

The first was described by one of the *Homo habilis* century's most influential thinkers, the Swiss psychologist Carl Gustav Jung. He defined synchronicity as any apparent coincidence that inspires a sense of wonder and personal meaning or particular significance in an observer. It is a perceived connection between two or more objects, events, or persons without any recognizable cause. He used the term for the first time in 1930 to describe a situation in which apparently unrelated events converge to form a shared experience regarded as momentous by the person experiencing it. At a decisive moment in her treatment, a female client was describing a vividly recollected dream in which someone presented her with a costly piece of jewelry fashioned in the image of a scarab beetle. She was a particularly troublesome case—"psychologically inaccessible," according to Jung—a young person whose strongly narrow view of the world admitted no reality beyond that which was not immediately and physically perceptible and rationally acceptable. Because of her unswerving, materialistic mindset, her treatment had come to an impasse. But as she related her dream of the golden scarab, Jung heard a distinct tapping at the window. He saw that the sound was being made by a large insect that seemed intent on getting inside. Jung opened the window and caught the creature as it flew past him, then gave it to his patient with the words "Here is your scarab."

In her hands she held a scarabaeid beetle, its gold-green color nearly matching the golden scarab jewel of her dream. The dumbfounded woman's exclusively rationalistic worldview was severely shaken, so much so that she was at last open to further treatment, which eventually concluded with positive results. The meaningful coincidence had no less a profound effect on Jung himself; it led him to his pioneering investigation of synchronicity. He noted that no beetle had ever before or since made such a racket at his window. In fact, he could not even remember seeing an insect of this kind so late in the season. An old, central European folk belief holds that if a beetle flies into one's house, it is an omen of unexpected news. But in Egyptian mythology, the insect is better known. Scarabs were emblems of Khepera, seen in the morning sun, daily confirmation of his function as the god of resurrection. His name means at once "Scarab" and "He Who Becomes," or "The Becomer." Living beetles were looked upon as his physical incarnation, so Egyptians wore scarab amulets to attract Khepera's regenerative power. Remarkably, in her dream, Jung's patient was presented with a scarab amulet that, in her waking state, summoned its animal counterpart (or so the ancient Egyptians would have believed). And the meeting of the subconscious symbol with its biological object generated in her a powerful regenerative change for the better, the kind of born-again experience that characterized Khepera, "The Becomer." Joseph Campbell, the great American mythologist, who devoted his life to studying Jung's subconscious correlation of myth, experienced his own appropriate synchronicity. Living in New York City at the time, he was intensely studying a book on Bushman mythology, in which the praying mantis plays the hero's role. In the midst of his reading, Campbell felt a sudden urge to open the window. As he did so, he was flabbergasted to see the largest praying mantis he had ever encountered crawling along the rim. As he studied it more closely, the insect swiveled its head and looked directly at the astonished scholar.

"His face looked just like a Bushman's face," Campbell recalled. The statistical improbability of this meaningful coincidence was heavily underscored by the apartment's location fourteen floors above 6th Avenue, an unlikely place to find such a large specimen. Interestingly, Campbell's synchronicity bears an uncanny resemblance to that experienced by Jung, who had been similarly greeted by a timely insect at his window, itself an archetype. He also relates an instance of avian synchronicity typical of its kind.

The wife of one of his patients recounted how birds flocked around the windows of the room in which her mother lay dying. Her grandmother's death was accompanied by the same phenomenon. Years later, a medical specialist sent the woman's husband home with a clean bill of health, but when he came home his wife was horrified to see a flock of birds suddenly descend on their house. Aware that similar appearances had coincided with the deaths of her mother and grandmother, she felt the nearness of some impending tragedy. Shortly thereafter, her husband unexpectedly collapsed with a heart attack in the street and was brought home very close to death.

Birds signify spiritual transition, of which dying is only one kind. They do seem to imply the soul taking leave of its physical home, especially if a window plays some part in their appearance. According to the Spanish symbolist J. E. Cirlot, the window expresses penetration and distance, with terrestrial implications, as well as consciousness. Hence, the birds, as living metaphors of the soul's flight toward the spiritual Otherworld, beckon through the window of the mundane world, an aperture in our physical existence through which the soul must leave.

But birds are also traditionally regarded as messengers of heavenly favor. When, for example, the boy Claudius Germanicus happened to catch a little puppy dropped from the talons of a huge black eagle flying overhead, a visiting priest who witnessed the incident declared on the spot that the youngster would someday rule Rome. The priest's interpretation was met with general derision, because the lad appeared to be a stuttering moron. Even so, some forty years later, he became Emperor Claudius.

Stories about dogs, being common household pets, abound of their often-uncanny synchronous behavior and interactions with their human companions. A typical example took place around the dinner table of Minnesota publisher Phyllis Galde one evening. She was telling me that her big husky, Ivan, who was attentively watching her speak, had once devoured a candle. "Would you do that again?" she asked him. I seemed to read either his mind or the expression on his face and spoke for him, saying, "Try me!"

Also sitting at the table was her editor, David Godwin, previously lost in thought, who suddenly looked up in surprise. He said we had all just participated in a synchronicity that only he recognized. Immediately previous to and during our discussion about Ivan's preference for candles, David was seriously considering a problem his Masonic lodge was having with candles for a second-degree ceremony to be conducted the following evening. Not only that, but at the precise moment I spoke for Ivan, David thought of the ritual response given by an initiate in the candle ceremony, which is "Try me!"

While writing *Our Dolphin Ancestors*, I was struck by the sea mammal's highly developed telepathic sense. An almost typical instance occurred at a coastal Florida ocean park in 1997. A long, narrow channel had been dug inland, providing the dolphins a direct outlet to the sea, while visitors could get a close view of them in shallow water. One morning, a small crowd of tourists were walking along the banks of the channel, when a single, medium-sized, female dolphin gently tossed a small pebble from the tip of its snout at one of the women visitors. The pebble hit the woman softly on her stomach, to everyone's amusement.

They were amazed, however, when the dolphin reappeared to launch another well-aimed pebble at the same woman, striking her harmlessly again on the stomach. Going for a third time, the woman stood facing the edge of the water, waiting for the dolphin's return. A few moments later, it resurfaced and flung yet another tiny stone accurately at the woman's midsection. "What could have caused it to act so strangely?" wondered the tour director, who had never seen such dolphin behavior before. "Well," the targeted visitor blushed, "she knew something no one else knows, but I was recently made aware of. My doctor told me just yesterday that I'm pregnant."

May these few synchronicities slightly crack open the door to *Mysterious Messages from Beyond* that Von Braschler throws wide for all his readers!

Frank Joseph
Author of *Our Dolphin Ancestors* and *Synchronicity as Mystical Experience*

INTRODUCTION

Did you ever pick up the phone but find it impossible to make sense of some strange message or inexplicable voice at the other end? Did you ever walk through woods alone and hear your name ring out eerily with nobody in sight? Did you ever lie in bed in the early morning and try to make sense of strange voices that called out numbers or words that only you likely heard? Well, maybe all of that was really more than just your idle imagination. Maybe these were strange messages from beyond, intended just for you.

If you ever received bizarre messages directed your way or else heard from friends who did, then this book is for you. It is a collection of true-life accounts of people like you who have received curious phone calls or other communication that could not be easily explained. These are stories like the little secrets you might be harboring or tales that loved ones or neighbors have confided with a shake of their confused heads.

We've all heard these sorts of disjointed stories, most likely. Sometimes we don't talk about them with others, because they sound implausible or just plain crazy. We might convince ourselves finally that these odd messages from beyond are likely delusions or else projections of a desire to hear from deceased loved ones or receive insightful prompts from a higher source.

For everyone who has admitted to receiving such strange messages from beyond or heard from others who believe they did, there are undoubtedly many times more people who keep this sort of odd occurrence to themselves. They simply choose not to acknowledge it or give it any credence or disregard the voices they thought they heard. This book is about them too.

As a trained journalist who has learned to report and try to make sense of communication, I have compiled some representative stories of people just like you who sometimes hang up the phone because what they heard makes no sense. I have personally experienced strange messages from beyond, unearthly voices that cannot be easily explained. I also have interviewed and known other people with similar stories that left them shaking their heads.

So this is not a scientific study or even a survey of a cross section of people. It is a book of real people who claim they received strange messages from beyond that they cannot readily explain. I don't ask you to take them at their word, but to consider whether you have heard anything like their personal tales and whether there seems to be a pattern to all of this.

In assessing these odd stories of unusual communication, I will try to determine how they occur, why they happen, and how we should respond when strange calls like that come our way.

I was trained by a renowned psychic, the late author Louis Gittner, to focus my listening. He told me that not all voices are easily recognized. He told me to always remember three things: listen, listen, and listen. He even wrote a book with that title.

Under his direction, I learned to hear and see ghosts and speak to spirits (not something I enjoy doing much these days but have done when necessary). He showed me how to hear helpful spirits from beyond who want only to impart advice and direction. He taught me how to see with new eyes and hear with new ears.

For a lot of people, however, a strange message from beyond can be jarring and confusing. It can even prove frightening and leave you questioning your sanity.

This book attempts to make some sense of that. It considers the communication process as more than simply a physical message, a communication conveyance, and an exchange between a focused sender and a willing, attentive listener. It examines the role of invisible thought forms and the power of thought and the energy waves created by consciousness. It examines the focus, intent, and purpose behind thought transference and the limitless energy waves of thought when projected by focused consciousness.

1

A HISTORY OF
MYSTERIOUS CALLS

There is a rich history of mysterious calls from beyond—mostly involving ghostly phone calls. Even Thomas Edison considered how to get calls from beyond on his new invention and made plans for a special phone with that special purpose. Early telegraphs and phones often seemed to capture spirit communication, and spiritualists in the early twentieth century focused on building the right apparatus to talk to the mysterious callers.

On some occasions, however, our everyday phones ring with phantom messengers that defy logical explanation. Sometimes the caller is someone we seem to recognize from a distant past, and sometimes the caller is a total mystery to us. Almost always, these mysterious calls can't be verified because they are very personal—aimed at just one person. And these events are almost always anecdotal, a tall tale told by the exasperated person who received the call and can't really convince anyone that it happened that way.

This book includes a lot of new stories. These are personal encounters that happened to me and people I know personally. Some of the stories here, however, will not include a telephone. It is my contention that spirit communication comes in many forms but tends to utilize electronic communication devices.

To put these modern stories in context, it's useful here to consider the historical pattern of mysterious calls that have been recorded. I have tracked them back to the start of the telegraph and telephone, up to a modern account verified in a scholarly report by Kathryn Ramsland, PhD. She is a respected author and professor of forensic psychology who reported on a mysterious phone call made to bestselling author Dean Koontz in 1988. Dr. Ramsland reviews the famous novelist's strange encounters in her book *Dean Koontz: A Writer's Biography* (1997). Her research into the strange calls that Koontz received have been verified by *Psychology Today* magazine and were posted online by the magazine on September 27, 2013.

Koontz picked up the phone in his office when it rang one day. A female voice warned him to be careful. He asked the caller to identify herself, but she did not. She repeated the warning three times, each time her voice becoming more distant. She spoke with urgency. Then the line went dead. Apparently, Koontz thought the voice sounded like his mother, who had died two years earlier. Later, Koontz visited his psychologically troubled father, who wrestled with him and apparently brandished a knife during the encounter. Afterward, Koontz reflected again on the mysterious phone warning to be careful.

Koontz subsequently wrote about his mysterious call in an essay called "Beautiful Death" as possible evidence of life after death. The subsequent incident with his ailing father he included in a scene in his 1993 novel *Mr. Murder*.

But phantom phone calls have been ringing in people's ears from the first crank phones to the cell phones we use today. Sometimes the phones ring, even when they were not properly installed or connected.

REPEATED CALLS FROM A TRAIN CRASH VICTIM

Callen Cooper in his wonderful book *Telephone Calls from the Dead* recounts an amazing series of phone calls from a man who died in a train crash in 2008. On September 12, 2008, a Metrolink and Union Pacific freight train collision in California killed many people, apparently including Charles Peck, age forty-nine. Peck's phone continued to dial his family after his believed demise, however. Peck's mobile phone dialed his son at the time of the crash and dialed his family several times during the site recovery period. Each time, the family could hear only static on the line. When the family tried calling his cell phone back after these calls, the calls went straight to his voicemail. Thinking that Peck was somehow alive, the family encouraged rescuers to reach for his body. When they found him, however, it was determined that he had died on first impact and had been dead for some time. The calls finally stopped half an hour after a recovery team found Peck's body. Some thirty-five calls came from this dead man's phone after the crash, yet the mobile phone itself was never found.

Dr. Cooper also chronicles how wireless telegraph in the early 1900s produced mysterious calls from beyond many times. Some of these reports from mediums and other paranormal enthusiasts might not be legitimate messages, but apparently some cannot be easily dismissed.

Londoner David Wilson in 1913 heard of telegraphic messages from the spirit realm and began experimenting with a wireless telegraph that reportedly received Morse code signals from mysterious sources, according to Cooper's excellent book.

Francis Grierson in his 1921 book *Psycho-Phone Messages* describes ghostly voices on what Dr. Cooper calls an interdimensional telephone. Grierson referred to "psycho-phonic waves" in his book, received by wireless methods. These earlier reports created a sensation and led to other efforts to capture messages from beyond.

British paranormal researcher F. R. Melton built a psychic telephone to contact the dead and reported his results in a 1921 booklet called *A Psychic Telephone*. He even took his device into churches to allow people an opportunity to speak to their dead loved ones.

EVEN EINSTEIN AND ALEXANDER GRAHAM BELL WERE INVOLVED

There is some evidence that even Albert Einstein was interested in spirit communication, and Alexander Graham Bell showed interest in designing another telephone that would talk to the dead after seeing what he believed to be photographs of spirits. He believed it likely that the dead might want to contact their relatives and needed a way to do so, but he died in 1931 before building his ghost phone.

Dr. Cooper's book on telephone calls from the dead builds on the classic book by his heroes, Raymond Bayless and D. Scott Rogo, who wrote so many articles on proof of survival for the American digest *FATE* magazine. Rogo and Bayless researched many reports on spirit communication in their classic book *Phone Calls from the Dead.*

After two years of research, they concluded that these enigmatic phone calls do occur and are probably more common than most people might imagine. They further stated that people who report such incidents are not perpetrating hoaxes but have genuine experiences that most parapsychologists have generally ignored. They characterized these phantom phone calls as just another form of psychic communication.

Psychic experiments with spirit communication continued in the 1940s, '50s, and '60s and have been studied by authors William Hall and Jimmy Petonito, who followed these incidents up to modern day. They analyzed more-recent reports of chilling communications in everything from emails to texts, letters, and phone calls in their book *Phantom Messages.*

In reviewing many compelling cases, they discovered that twenty-two of them involved landline phones, ten involved cell phone calls or texts, ten involved radio, seven involved computers, five appeared on voicemail, four came across television, three came over speakers, two came through cable boxes, and two came through letters. It seems that the spirit world is trying very hard to break through to communicate with some of us and will resort to any means available.

Many of these mysterious messages came from relatives and a few from friends, but more than half came from unknown entities or extraterrestrials, according to their excellent research.

Some were warnings, predictions, or calls for help. Others simply disconnected or left no displayed or traceable number. In six of their studied cases, the caller simply said, "Hello."

Curiously, some involved routed calls. Some were long-distance calls. A few were related to time of death. In some cases, there was no record with the phone company that the call ever happened. In a few rare cases, the messages were quite long.

Lest you think such reports are cultural phenomena that happen only in certain settings, Hall and Petonito show how cases they studied in depth happened in various places around the world.

THE BEATLES HEAR FROM THE LATE JOHN LENNON

Some of the more interesting cases they studied include celebrities with otherworldly messages. Surviving Beatles Paul McCartney, George Harrison, and Ringo Starr gathered after the death of bandmate John Lennon to record "Free as a Bird" in a recording studio. From a disconnected speaker, they heard John Lennon commenting on the session. Apparently, they recorded his comment. In addition, they "sensed" his presence in the studio.

In pointing out the timelessness of the spirit realm, Hall and Petonito also discuss time slips in spirit communication. One intriguing case comes from a disconnected pool phone at a haunted apartment building that had once been a hospital and nursing home. Shadowy figures appeared briefly before a man when he was awakened by the call. In the same haunted building, a tenant reportedly heard himself dying when he answered the phone and heard a loud-beating heart and a respirator. Two months later, that call proved prophetic when the man died of a sudden heart attack.

We must remember the general intent of all communication to deliver messages that are personally directed to specific targets in an apparent attempt to convey information. We know that determined people will find a way to communicate when a message must be delivered. We communicate psychically all the time by sending thought forms. Often, we use body language or verbal communication. We use whatever works and whatever is needed. We use whatever means a person at the receiving end might recognize. Most of us are accustomed to receiving communication from distant, unseen sources on a phone, so using something that common and convenient would seem reasonable.

We are now accustomed to turning to television, radio, text messaging, and the internet to receive messages from distant, unseen callers; therefore, it stands to reason that determined communicators with an urge to reach us should approach us in these recognized channels.

A ham radio operator in 2015, according to the Hall and Petonito study, found her deceased father's old ham radio in an attic and turned it on. M. J. Carcuro of Schenectady, New York, waited patiently for the old tubes to warm up after plugging it in. Then she was surprised to hear her father's voice very clearly saying to her, "Hello, Pumpkin!" It was his childhood nickname for the daughter he loved even beyond the grave. She ran downstairs to get her husband as a witness. When she returned, her husband heard the unmistakable voice too. It repeated the greeting. M. J. asked her father if he was okay. "Yes," he responded. Then she asked him if her deceased mother was there with him. "Yes," he answered her. Then they heard only static, followed by silence on the radio. Hall and Petonito conclude that electromagnetic energy enables paranormal activity. That would seem most obvious in electronic communication, seemingly a favorite route for phantom callers and the media they select as a conveyance.

2

RADIO MESSAGES
WITHOUT ANY RADIO

Over the years, I have personally experienced strange messages from beyond and have known people close to me who have received phantom messages too. Since such case studies are anecdotal and very personal stories, I figure the ones that I know firsthand or secondhand are the stories I can most reliably relate to you. Certainly, these are the most intimate and detailed stories that I know.

The first phantom message that I can personally recall was a radio program. It seemed like a radio signal aimed only at me. I was approximately thirteen years old when I heard it in my backyard in Everett, Washington.

I remember this very distinctly because I had never experienced anything quite like it. I was lying on my back on the summer grass, looking up at the sun and shielding my eyes. It was a beautiful, clear day with blue sky and sunshine. It was quiet there in the yard, and I was alone with my thoughts. I had just taken a break from practicing my fly casting, as taught to me by my neighbor who was an ardent fisherman in his retirement from a career as a butcher. He would give me his copies of *Outdoor Life* magazine and show me how to become proficient in fly casting. He lived to fish. I just thought that it was fun to try to perfect the sort of timing and precision to cast a line and drop it 30 yards in front of you with a gentle, even landing. With arms tired from practice, I reclined on my back and enjoyed the tranquility of a summer day alone in my yard. I was inside a wooden fence that enclosed our grassy yard to the side of our house. Our one-and-a-half-story white house, a 1940s bungalow, had a side door that connected our side yard to the kitchen. What I remember about that summer day was how pleasant it was outside. There was little wind, with clear skies and warm weather, and it was quiet. I was alone, with nobody around the house or anywhere near our house.

A RADIO BROADCAST FOR JUST ONE

Out of the blue, I began to receive what sounded like a radio signal. It sounded just like a local Top 40 station, but the source of the music I heard was eerie. I listened for a while and decided that the sound was more inside my head than outside my head. It was as though the signal was aimed only at me or heard only by me. I did not feel the watchful eyes of my neighbor looking down upon me from his upstairs window in the house next door. I heard nobody out from beyond the fence to our yard or from the side street. Behind our backyard was an empty garage. I recall standing up and looking over my backyard fence to determine if there was a logical explanation beyond my sight. Maybe there was a radio somewhere or some physical source of the sound somewhere nearby. I found nothing. In fact, when I stepped outside the backyard and into the front yard, the sound subsided. I returned to the backyard and looked around there. The nearby door to the house was closed, and no windows were open. There was nobody inside the house at that time, in fact. I was the last person in the house, and there was no radio, television, or music source playing there when I went outdoors. No, the sound had no obvious, physical source that I could determine. But yet I could hear it distinctly. The song I heard was instrumental. It was not my memory playing a favorite song over and over, because I didn't recognize the song exactly. In time, that song gave way to a new song. I remember giving up on trying to find a logical source for the music in my head. So, I just focused on the music. If I concentrated, I could tune it in better so that the signal was clearer and a little louder. I was convinced that nobody but me could hear this music. And I just enjoyed the show, since it appeared to be aimed personally at me. I must have reclined on my back on the grass on that quiet, summer day for thirty minutes or longer, listening to my music, wondering if it would ever end. Song after song played. I decided just to enjoy the moment and not try to analyze it; there seemed to be no way to analyze it. Nothing like this had ever happened to me before, and I doubted that anyone would believe me if I tried to describe what I was hearing on my own.

A BUS FAR FROM TOWN

The summer before, I had boarded a converted school bus and gone berry picking with other kids from my old neighborhood. I had never ridden on a yellow school bus before, so the whole ride sounded like fun that long summer. My neighborhood friends who normally played ball, rode bikes, or went swimming with me that summer had all decided to visit a berry field outside our town to pick strawberries for pocket money. There was literally nobody to play with me, so I hopped on the berry bus too. I didn't work hard picking berries, honestly. As I recall, I would pick a few in the morning just to eat off the vine. Then I would go to the swimming hole at the river, where kids often went during their lunch break. I would get there early, stay beyond lunch, and swim much of the afternoon. In all the days I went there, I think I made at most a dollar one day. Mostly I just ate some berries, went swimming, and enjoyed the bus ride. It was something to do for a few weeks that summer.

One day, however, I developed a troublesome pain in my abdomen in the morning. I stopped eating berries, thinking I had eaten too many and upset my stomach. I went to the swimming hole but did not eat my lunch. My abdomen hurt too much. When my friends showed up at the swimming hole during the lunch break, I told them I felt pretty sick and wanted to go home early. They suggested that I talk to the bus driver about an early ride home. The bus driver asked the owner of the berry field and determined that I would need to wait until the end of the day to ride back with the others. The driver suggested that I just sit quietly and wait. Maybe I would feel better if I just rested, he said. But the pain only increased. I decided that I needed to leave somehow.

I stood by the bus, staring down the road. I knew that I was out of town and didn't know the way back. Besides, it was a good half-hour ride by bus, so it was quite a distance from my home. I just felt that I needed to get home quickly, because the deep pain in my abdomen was something I had never experienced before and something I sensed was very dangerous.

Then I noticed the train track near the berry field. We crossed the train tracks every day coming into the field and leaving the field. The road into the field was built over these train tracks. I tried to remember how often I heard a train on these tracks. It seemed to come very seldom during the day. I considered following the train tracks home. Would these tracks lead to my home? I tried to figure it out, but I was becoming too sick to think clearly.

At last, I concluded that train tracks were in front of my home, so the tracks should lead me right to my front door. Looking back now, that was a huge stretch of my young imagination to think that. I had no idea where these particular tracks led. Train tracks have switches and go in all different directions. But in desperation, I mounted the tracks and began walking away from the berry field. It was fairly early in the day. I hoped that the tracks would get me home by later in the afternoon so that somebody would be home to take care of me, whatever that involved.

I remember looking back at everyone picking berries, oblivious to my sudden departure. Then I rounded a bend where tall stands of wild Himalayan blackberry bushes blocked my view of the berry field. I was on my way home. I tried to trust the plan, forget the gnawing pain in my abdomen, and focus only on maintaining a steady walking clip.

A MIRACULOUS RETURN HOME

Suddenly, I found myself in front of my home. It seemed almost instantaneous, which was miraculous, of course. It was even more miraculous when I looked back on it a year later, reclining on my back in the backyard and listening to music from beyond. At last I was able to sort out the crazy inconsistencies from a year ago. Maybe it was the tranquility of reclining on lovely summer grass and looking up at the sun and blue sky. Maybe it was the music out of the blue that jarred things loose at last. But I realized on that day that I could not possibly have walked the train tracks for miles and miles without any sense of direction as a young boy and found myself in front of my house in the blink of an eye. It would have required hours of strained walking in my weakened condition. It would have taken a knowledge of train tracks. And it would have required train tracks that actually led to my front door in the next town.

With a start, I rose to my feet in the backyard and walked into the front of the house, directed by a sudden realization. I had to stand there and stare at the startling reality with my own eyes, wide open. You see, the train tracks did not lead to my front door. In fact, the train tracks were nowhere near my house. The closest train tracks were halfway across town, a few miles away. Yet, my memory still told me that I had walked from the berry field in the next town in just a few minutes, following train tracks that magically led to my front door. I clearly remember stepping off the track and walking to the front door. My mother was not home. I remember opening the front door and looking for her. Then I remember collapsing on her bed, just beyond our living room on the first floor. My father was working out of town and not home that day. I waited for my mother to return, and tried to convince her that my bellyache was something quite serious, something I had never felt before and sensed was dangerous. She offered me some 7-Up to settle my stomach. When the pain was worse the next morning, she called our doctor, who advised us to get to the hospital for an appendectomy. Waiting for the doctor to arrive from the golf course where my mother had reached him that morning, my appendix burst in the operating room. But the surgery was successful, and I found myself back home soon in good shape again.

Strangely, my friends at the berry field do not recall seeing me leave, although I was not on their return bus that night. Nobody could explain my amazingly fast and efficient return home. Consequently, I stopped talking to people about it. I got home, had my appendix removed in time, and recovered nicely. Raising disturbing questions about how I got home only made me sound a little off in the head. And maybe that's how people resolved the story to their satisfaction. They probably figured that I was a little out of my head in my illness and could not accurately recount the real story of how I got home that day. I tried to wipe that inconsistency out of my head too. There was no logical, physical explanation that made sense.

While I kept details of my ordeal to myself, I nonetheless tried to make some sense of it to my own satisfaction, if only to put my mind to rest over the implausibility of the whole thing. I considered how I could have wandered home on my own in such a short time. I know that my long trip was quick, because I got home in the early afternoon, well ahead of my mother's return or the return of my siblings from school. That seemed totally unlikely. My return home was not only quick—virtually instantaneous—but also made on train tracks that clearly did not lead to my home. I started on train tracks and then found myself miraculously transported miles away to the door of my home.

I considered outside intervention. I had heard as a boy in church that an angel might come to your rescue and that Jesus would carry you if you were unable to walk. Frankly, I had never met anyone with this divine experience or heard anyone who remembered such a fortunate rescue. Then again, maybe I was unconscious or not fully conscious when I was transported home. In that case, outside intervention seemed possible and something I would not recall. Maybe aliens had taken me. But why would they take me home? And how would they know where I lived? People often speculate that they have been taken by aliens, but they generally talk about being taken elsewhere for study. Besides, I didn't think extraterrestrials would have particular interest in me. I started to think about time travel and how time and space are illusions. Could I have been instantaneously transported through time and space? The idea was intriguing.

I had no answers, only questions. But sometimes I think the questions might be more important than answers if you want to start your feet on the path of real learning.

So I tucked the incident away in my head and didn't bring it up with my friends and relatives.

A REALIZATION

A year later, I heard that amazing music and thought about how I had apparently walked home on mysterious train tracks the previous summer. When I suddenly remembered the strange ordeal the previous year, I was moved. I stood up and walked beyond the fence into our front yard. I tried to picture standing on the other side of the street on train tracks. I could still remember standing on train tracks outside my home, facing the front door. But now when I stood at the front of my house, I saw no tracks. I found myself staring at a row of houses instead. There was nothing even resembling train tracks there, I had to admit to myself. There never had been. Three years later, however, we moved from that house to the outskirts of the next town to the north. Curiously, the only way to reach this new house was to drive across train tracks. We lived on this private dirt road near the train tracks and had to cross the tracks every time we entered our driveway. When we moved there, we joked about living on the other side of the tracks. The joke was on me. Standing in front of my new home in the new town to the north, I could see the train tracks out front. These train tracks led right to my front door. But that was three years in the future from the day I walked home from the berry field, trusting that train tracks led to my front door.

I have tried to resolve the oddities in this personal story of survival. What does a kid know, anyway? Years later, however, I still cannot solve the puzzle. But it all seemed to come together for me in some strange way when I reclined on my back on the summer grass that one sunny day and heard radio music out of nowhere. The music seemed to jog something inside me. At the time I heard the music in my old backyard, I tried to rationalize how I could become a successful receptor of these radio signals. It seemed to me that the signal originated somewhere in the physical world and traveled through the airwaves to myself as a receptor. But what made me a receptor? I considered that the metal fillings in my teeth might have played a part. My dental fillings were the only part of my physical body that were not part of my original human makeup, and I reasoned that other human beings do not hear music inside their heads naturally. That might sound silly, but I was a young boy with limited scientific training. It did seem that the music occurred inside my head, however, and not outside my head. Over the many years from that day when I heard the music, I have given much more consideration to the puzzle. I toyed for a while with the romantic notion of old radio signals that travel endlessly through time and space as waves of vibrating energy.

Sometimes now I reflect on the electromagnetic energy all around us and how our bodies absorb and utilize this electromagnetic energy. From the sun above us to the very core of our world on this earth, electromagnetic radiation moves in wave action. Such radiant energy includes microwaves, infrared waves, light waves, ultraviolet waves, x-rays, gamma rays, and even radio waves. These electromagnetic waves are synchronized oscillations of electric and magnetic fields that propagate at the speed of light.

3

THE MAGIC FLUTE

I never expected to hear ethereal music again. I mean, I heard it once when I was thirteen. That music sounded like instrumental music played on a radio without narration, one song right after the other. It sounded like the music was inside my head and not outside me. That sounds like a once-in-a-lifetime experience, something that doesn't happen to most people even once. So I was shocked when something similar happened to me some twenty years later in another part of the world.

I was living on Mount Hood in Oregon in 1981. I lived in a new development called Brightwood along the pristine Salmon River. The dense forest area of Brightwood once housed seasonal Native American gatherings in the early days before white settlers tried building there. In the '60s, new residents there were surprised by the heavy spring runoff from the mountain and nearly perished when the river flooded. Brave firefighters from nearby Sandy, Oregon, dove into the icy water to save people.

My house in Brightwood was part of a new development built there after most people forgot about the flooding decades earlier. I learned about it only when I tried to buy flood insurance and was rejected for living in a floodplain. But I loved the woods along the river there and never saw flood conditions when I lived in Brightwood. I did have some unusual experiences by the river there, however. My experiences were auditory. I heard music out of this world.

A POWER SPOT

When I first moved there, I heard a lot of lore from some of my neighbors. I learned that the Native Americans considered it a sort of sacred spot, a power place. They would bury things in the ground near there as gifts to the earth. They would also apparently have vision quests there and would speak to the trees. I never met any of them. I just got the impression from the lore I heard about their gatherings that our spot on the mountain seemed to have some extra energy for them.

I did spend some time with an old man who wrote children's stories from inspiration he claimed to receive from an old tree that he called Omar. When I asked him to show me his tree, he brought me to a log near his house and offered me a seat. We both sat on the log, which he told me was Omar in his present stage of life. The log spoke to him on a deep level, he said, dictating stories that eventually found their way into the old man's children's tales. I suggested that the old tree on which we sat actually inspired him and gave him ideas, but the man insisted that the tree told him stories to pass along. Apparently, the old tree had seen a lot over a long life and wanted to impart its wisdom.

During the Oregon pioneer days, one of the major Oregon trails was the Barlow Trail, which followed a path near Brightwood. In fact, the old Barlow Trail was just outside the front door from my house. Since I worked as the publisher of the local newspaper, I had access to descriptions of the descendants of these pioneers. They traveled with their heavy wagons, with children and animals in tow. This section of the Barlow Trail was near the end of a long, arduous journey across the country. By the time they reached this point on Mount Hood, some of them scattered apple seeds and flower seeds along the path of their promised land. Years later, I could walk into the woods thereabouts and find their apple trees and wildflowers growing in the middle of the woods or along the road. Yes, the woods were magical. Some people reported seeing ghosts of those who made it only this far along the long Oregon trail. They continue to walk the woods and along the trail—or so the ghostly encounters seem to relate.

As a modern Brightwood resident in a new development along the old Barlow Trail, I used to take late-night walks or sometimes jogs up the road that was once the trail of these westward-bound settlers. It was a quiet, isolated trek on a road with very little traffic. The old Barlow Trail was now a paved road, but pretty much like the old pioneer trail. It was late at night, close to midnight, when I saw odd things there myself. Someone might term these odd sightings as ghostly. I don't know. I can only relate the way it appeared to me.

The first thing I saw was a somewhat translucent figure of a man in old, ragged clothes, sitting beside what looked like a broken-down wagon train. I would characterize his clothing as very out of date and dirty. He had a ragged beard and disheveled hair. His boots looked worn. He looked very tired and worn down, as though he could not stand or go any farther. But he looked peaceful where he sat to rest. I caught a glance of him out of the corner of my left eye, as I rounded a hill on the old road and was startled by what I thought I saw. It was surreal but had some definition. It was not totally solid, but I am only describing the figure I saw sitting beside an old wagon in bright moonlight. When I looked at it straight on, facing it to take it all in, the ghostly figure began to fade and then disappeared in front of my eyes. I have no way to prove this but can only say that my neighbors told me similar encounters—always seen without any collaborating witnesses.

GHOST DOG

The other ghostly encounter I experienced there on my late-night outings on the old Barlow Trail was something quite different. I saw a dog with fierce, orange eyes walking toward me. I was jogging up the Barlow Trail road that night. It was pretty bright, but not a full moon. As I reached that point on the road, there was a turn in the road, and I noticed flashing road barriers put on the right side of the road. I adjusted my path to go to the left around the lights. But when I drew near the flashing lights, I began to see what looked like a white bulldog moving toward me. He continued to walk directly at me, and I wondered what he was doing there. I had never seen this dog in our area before so did not recognize him or recall ever seeing a dog quite like him. As he drew close to me, I looked into his eyes and was startled by what I saw. His eyes glowed brightly with a color that I would say was somewhere in the range of an orange hue. Frankly, I found him to be frightening, and I wondered how I should respond to him when we passed on the road. When we reached each other on the road, I diverted my eyes and slowed to a walk without incident. A few seconds later, I stopped to turn around to see what had passed me. The dog had vanished.

In earlier books, I have tried to describe these odd encounters in these enchanted woods on Mount Hood but have never resolved the many questions they raise, or come to grips with them. They still weigh on me. I used to gather by the river on the empty lots before Brightwood became more densely developed. There were few houses there at that time. So, I cut through woods to the river and sometimes went wading. I enjoyed building a little sitting area at the edge of the river. The place was very quiet and beautiful. Once I built a sort of outdoor altar with rocks, driftwood, plants, and other natural elements in the area. I marked off the four corners to honor the four cardinal directions. When I finished, I consecrated the spot as my own power spot. When I finished, cumulus clouds over the river seemed to part to reveal a smiling face.

On that occasion, I felt like taking a walk downstream along the river. On my return trip, heading upstream, I felt inspired to enter the woods along the river. This was a section of woods downstream that I had not previously traveled. It was very dense with grouse and other wild creatures, not accustomed to seeing people there. I walked slowly and quietly. I was put into a special state of reverence from the outdoor altar consecration earlier. I remember how focused and intense I felt. I was in a state of superconsciousness, very alert and very attentive. As I walked through those woods, I seemed to see with wider eyes and keener ears. I noticed every little pine cone, twig, and branch. I heard every little chipmunk and bird. I seemed more alive and awake than ever. It was magical.

DISTANT MUSIC

Then something really magical happened. I started hearing some distant music somewhere there in the woods. It was faint at first, so I kept winding my way around trees and brush to get nearer to the source of the sound. It was a most unusual musical sound. I tried to tune in to the sound so that it was clearer and louder, but found that difficult. So I walked around and around in search of the sound. That did not seem to bring me any closer.

It was strange. The song was clearly outside me, and yet I could not determine the source to draw nearer. I focused intently on the sound and found that concentration on my part could somehow amplify the sound. At last, I could identify this beautiful, exotic music. It was a flute! But it was a flute unlike any other I had ever heard. It was simply out of this world. And the music of the flute was like no other music I had ever heard. It was a single flute that kept playing one elongated melody line. The melody was enchanting. I searched to find the music. I wanted to throw myself into it and wrap myself in its harmony. The music touched me on an intimate level deep within my soul. It triggered something, that's for certain. It seemed to transport me to another place, transforming my being. I wondered where that new place was. My instinct was to draw nearer to the source of the magical music, so that I could become one with this glorious sound. It seemed to register with me as vibrations that achieved a level of harmonic resonance. Everything seemed better when I heard it, as though I had reached a point of oneness with nature and some divine plan that delivered me to my true soul's purpose and destiny. So, I wandered throughout the dense woods, not so much watching out for branches in my way but following the sound and trying to bring it closer. It seemed in my wandering that I could enhance the flute's sweet sounds with some turns I made, as though I was drawing nearer. But my level of heightened consciousness in trying to hold the music in my head and tune in to it seemed to be the real key to any success.

It occurred to me that the music was all around me and inside me, as though I had been transported to some magical environment where the music permeated anything and everything that was receptive to hearing its beauty. Since this happened in tranquil, isolated woods beside the river on a perfect summer day, I wondered whether I had entered an enchanted forest. After all, this is where the Native Americans gathered for visionary rituals on a regular seasonal basis. The woods inspired my neighbors. Was I channeling something that played through the trees like a magical musical elixir?

The flute was somewhat alien to me and my limited knowledge of music at that time. I don't recall hearing flute music prior to that day that sticks out in my mind, except perhaps for some blues-rock music I might have incidentally encountered in the '60s and '70s. That sort of electric flute music didn't do much for me either way. This etheric music I heard that day on the mountain was completely different from that sort of flute music or any other I had ever heard, including classical flute. This mysterious music was enchanting.

BECOMING A BETTER RECEIVER

Realizing at last that my wandering through the woods would not bring me closer to the music, I simply stopped walking altogether. I focused on concentrating on the music and heightening my consciousness. That seemed to be what best connected me to the music. When I focused on the music and cleared my mind of any other considerations, the music seemed to become clearer and louder inside me. I could make myself a better receiver.

I focused only on the sound, clearing my mind of any other thoughts or impressions. I tuned out all internal dialogue and processing of information. I tuned out all external distractions. I no longer heard the birds in the woods or noticed the many little creatures crawling throughout the forest. I no longer saw the moss, ferns, pine cones, or trees. I closed my eyes and tuned in to the music only.

In this way, I seemed to reach a higher level of consciousness, a level of superconsciousness where I had a heightened awareness of my intended focus—the music. I turned my full intention to bringing the music to me, without any interference, buffering, or filtering. The world around me stopped, with my perception turned down. I tuned out everything except my awareness of the music as my only focus. You might accurately refer to this state of heightened awareness as a deep meditation. I was connecting with the signal I was receiving—the sound of the music.

I listened to it intently for several amazing minutes, allowing the majesty of the mystical music to roll over me as waves of energy that restored my soul. This wasn't music in the usual sense, but some kind of communication that seemed to be directed at me. I had to wonder who or what directed it. Who sent the music my way? All effective communication has a dedicated sender, a willing receptor, a message, and a reliable medium to deliver that message. I was a willing receptor. I could not begin to comprehend the medium that delivered the music to me. It seemed to ride on the wind. Since my consciousness seemed to be deeply involved in the efficient delivery of the message, I had to conclude that consciousness was the medium or at least a part of it or a way of thinking of it. Consciousness is still so mysterious to us, although we employ it every day in many ways. Apparently, it can be fine-tuned and heightened in the way an antenna brings in a signal.

WHO'S BEHIND THE MUSIC?

But what about the sender? Who or what was sending me this music, and for what purpose? It did seem to inspire me, enrich me, and wash over me like pulses of revitalizing energy. All energy involves vibration, and music most certainly has vibration that can be measured. But I doubted that I could measure these waves; they appeared not to be physical in the way we think of the physical world in terms of materialism. I was not hearing simply with my ears. So, hearing didn't involve my sensory perceptions as part of my physical being.

The longer I listened in this state of heightened consciousness, the more I began to visualize who or what was behind the music. I believe that I turned off my analytical mind in my deep meditative state. A picture began to form inside me on a blank slate before my mind's eye. The more the music played, the more the picture formed and assumed shape and definition. I saw a Pan-like figure, a sort of pied piper playing a flute in the woods. This is something in our mythology, of course, the god of the forest who plays the magical flute and directs the magical movements of woodland spirits. I know it sounds strange, but I began to see a hairy, horned being with cloven hooves and a panpipe in his hands. It was not a flute of the sort we see in the orchestra or a bandstand today. It was a set of pipes that he played. And it was beautiful.

This sounds fanciful and a bit imaginative on my part, of course. But that's what came to mind. Perhaps I visualized Pan with panpipes because I came to realize that the music that I heard sounded more like pipes than a flute. Maybe I visualized what sort of creature would be playing pipes of this sort, and that did not bring to mind a jazz musician or classical musician in an orchestra. It is possible, too, that the image was planted in my mind and did not spring from any active imagination. Maybe the image was sent to me in the same way the music was sent to me. It is difficult to imagine what someone speaking to you looks like when your eyes are closed. I just know that when I opened my eyes and returned to normal consciousness, with the overload of every form of stimulus around me, that the music began to fade. And when I walked out of those enchanting woods, the music died. Whatever magic was there is probably still there, if anyone could find the quiet space within themselves to hear it. But there is no way I can ever forget the music I heard that summer day.

4

LEARNING TO LISTEN

One of my first teachers was a psychic author named Louis Gittner. He gave me three rules to follow in order to plug into the greater world around me, the unseen world. The first rule he gave me was to listen. The second was to listen. And the third, also, was to listen.

Maybe Louis thought some of his students would forget his three rules along the way, now that he has passed. To help us remember, he wrote a book aptly titled *Listen, Listen, Listen*. Certainly, Louis lived what he taught. He was an excellent listener and heard mysterious messages from beyond all the time. His accomplishments in this role have been well outlined in a book by Brad Steiger titled *Words from the Source: A Metaphysical Anthology of Readings from the Louis Foundation*. I was fortunate to speak with Brad about his biography of Louis before Brad's own passing, to combine his impressions with my own intimate memories of lessons from Louis.

Louis would go into a deep meditation and hear strange messages that nobody near him could hear. He could do this while walking in his gardens around the Outlook Inn, where everything seemed to grow to amazing size and beauty. I once asked him about his unusual success in gardening, and he spoke about his intimate relationship with "energies," as he called them. These spirits communicated with him. He never called them nature spirits or faeries or anything specific. He always spoke in general terms about the energies who assisted him.

SAME MESSAGES RECEIVED AT FINDHORN

Curiously, Louis once told me that he considered the amazing success of gardeners at Findhorn to parallel his own experiences there on his island. He kept a sort of diary of his deep trances in which he received information. He wondered if the transmissions he received from unseen sources would match the special communication that gardeners at Findhorn received. Findhorn's gardens were amazing, and residents there insisted that they had special help from nature divas who communicated with them about their environment. Louis said that he was initially disappointed to learn that his transmissions from his energies didn't match up perfectly with the transmissions received from nature divas at Findhorn. They were similar messages and came on the same day but were several hours apart. So, he concluded initially that they were not receiving simultaneous transmissions from the unseen world. Then a realization dawned on him. Adjusting for the difference in time zones that separated them, the messages transmitted to Louis in the San Juan Islands came at precisely the same time as the messages delivered to Findhorn.

Typically, Louis would recline on his back in a room with shades drawn, sometimes with people around him to witness his communications and record his words. Louis would enunciate for the source of his communication, stating clearly in his own voice what messages came through to him. Curiously, his persona would change when he did verbalize the messages, using words and phrases that were not typical of his daily patterns of speech. It was as though he had become the unseen messengers who spoke through him.

Lest you label Louis as a medium, I should tell you that he admonished me to avoid dabbling in personal voyages to the spirit realm. He referred to that as a confused train station with many parties arriving and departing with cloaked identities. He cautioned me to avoid getting on strange trains and meeting strangers in this manner. It was unreliable, he said, and you couldn't always determine who was speaking to you or what their intentions were.

Louis knew his sources. They spoke to him frequently and intimately. He had merged with them, and they became part of his life and his moving reality. They came to him in light. One reason the shades were drawn when witnesses sat with Louis during his trancelike meditations was to block out the outside light and darken the room. Assistants reported a light coming out of nowhere during these meditation sessions and descending upon the chest of Louis during the communication process. There was no explanation for this strange light, but it accompanied the presence of his messengers.

Louis encouraged me to listen to the unseen world around me, putting myself into a meditative state ready to hear. He taught me that you can hear in ways other than with your ears. Exercises he gave me advanced that early training.

One thing he encouraged me to do during a visit to his island was to visit his little chapel in back of the inn. It was essentially a log cabin built from logs that he had transported to the island from the mainland on Washington State. Inside the little chapel were wooden benches in rows. He held Sunday morning services there. He told me to visit the chapel late at night and just sit there and wait to see who might visit me. These directions were given to me after I asked him how I could meet the energies that visit him. He told me to patiently wait there in the dark in a meditative state and to be very alert. He said that they might show up at around midnight.

MEETING SPIRITS IN A CHAPEL

I remember sitting there in the dark. I was with others who had accompanied me to the island. We sat patiently and waited. When you meditate, you seem to experience time in a different way. Waiting in the darkness there late at night, it seemed that we were there for hours. In reality, we were there only a few minutes. Just when I was about to go, thinking the possible moment had passed, a startling thing happened. Seated as I was, unobstructed and facing the front of the building, I saw little lights darting through the cracks in the logs piled atop each other to form a log-cabin wall. The tiny lights moved with an intelligence through the cracks and then changed directions to zigzag across the room. There were several of them. They darted toward me and the others seated there, and then swerved around us on a hurried path toward the back of the building. When we turned around to see where the tiny lights had gone after passing us, it was surprising how quickly they had disappeared. Apparently, they passed through the building from one end and exited through the other end rather quickly. I was elated! It seemed obvious to me that they were light beings with intelligence and purpose. They moved freely and with apparent intent and direction. They entered the building, zigzagged energetically, and then exited the building. And the whole thing took only a second or two.

The next morning, I related my success to Louis in the dining room at his inn. He smiled and told me how good it was that I had been able to see these energies. Then he asked me a troubling question. He wanted to know what I said to them. I stared at him dumbfounded. It had never occurred to me to open a dialogue with the energies or ask them anything. I was delighted just to see them for myself. Louis smiled and told me that was a shame and that I had missed an opportunity. But I see now that there are many such opportunities for us, if we learn to listen and become good receptors.

It is hard to really listen if we are always speaking. And it is hard to listen to outside voices if we are processing thoughts inside us all the time, never allowing a quiet time of tranquility and openness. Most of us are preoccupied with our own thoughts, processing analytical thought of unresolved events or concerns in our past or thoughts about the uncertainty of our future. We are self-absorbed and busy with a lot of noise inside us. When we cease these internal thoughts, it's generally to engage others around us when we speak. When do we set aside time to seriously listen? I would suggest that everyone needs to dedicate time for deep meditation. When we enter deep meditation, we can open ourselves to a vast universe of voices that might seek us out. If these outside messengers continually get a busy signal at our end, they simply don't get through with a message.

BASIC COMMUNICATION

So, let us look at what we basically need for effective communication. It requires a sender, receiver, message, and medium. But there are basic standards or qualifications for each of those four elements to meet.

A dedicated receptor (or listener) is necessary for effective communication. The role of the listener is not only critical, but essential. Whoever or whatever sends the communication might initiate the process and attempt to convey a message in the strongest terms that are easy to hear and comprehend. The message might have meaning and substance that makes it hard to ignore. The medium might be solid and reliable. But there must be a reliable receptor at the other end for the process to be effectively competed.

If nobody is really listening, then nothing is actually heard, and nothing is conveyed. The listener must be focused, open, and receptive. The listener must have attentive ears. That is basic for all effective communication. It would be true on any level, even when physical ears are not what is really needed. Consequently, it would be true of communication that occurs on a nonphysical level. We exist on many levels in addition to our physical bodies. Anyone who has seriously studied heightened consciousness and meditation is probably a little familiar with Eastern spiritual science. In the Hindu tradition, the holistic view of our being is multilayered. Our whole being includes subtle energy bodies that surround our core essence or physical body. Even modern Western science now looks at the interrelationship of the components of our being. We see the emotional body as affecting the physical body, and the mental body also affecting us on many levels. We see our etheric double as a thin outer shell to the physical body that acts almost as a membrane from our outer etheric bodies to our dense material body. We see a causal body that transcends the physical realm of cause and effect and gives us insight and creative focus. We see higher spiritual bodies that give us a sense of individuality and self-realization and a connection to the greater cosmos.

THE GREAT CONNECTION

Above all, we have a natural connection to divinity that transcends everything we experience in our mundane experiences in this lifetime. Sometimes the energy bodies that extend outside our physical bodies are seen as surrounding us and wrapping us in a webbing of light. You might think of them as our outer blankets, since they cover us. But they are also aspects of our total being, just as our physical body is one part of our total being.

We are complex beings, with energy bodies that connect us to various planes of existence. Each of our subtle energy bodies, while invisible to the eye, is a substantial aspect of our being. Each one corresponds to a nonphysical plane of existence and connects us to that plane. Each subtle energy body is a complete body unto itself and self-contained. It has its own chakras or power center that gives it energetic life. It operates on its corresponding level of existence. It offers us a portal to that plane of reality, where we have a seat at the table.

The most significant question for most of us, of course, is how to realize our place in these other realms of existence. We are fully equipped to occupy a place on the mental plane, spiritual plane, emotional plane, or spiritual planes. Only a fully self-realized person with an awareness of our cosmic position in the creation can live freely in all of these realms. Most of us ignore our full potential or receive only token impressions from our subtle energy bodies. We try to integrate these subtle energy bodies to more fully augment our physical selves. That benefits our physical body but does little if anything to develop our outer energy bodies.

Maybe it helps to think of the total human being with our subtle energy bodies by picturing an onion. Have you ever peeled down an onion, layer by layer, wondering which layers are nonessential? Maybe you peeled away several outer layers to get to a core that you considered the real essence of the onion. This is probably the way most people disregard their outer energy bodies, as unnecessary layers. But our outer energy bodies can connect us to unseen worlds of reality that most people have never even imagined. Everything that exists on these subtle energy bodies is nonphysical, of course, so we tend to disregard these bodies whatsoever. We have been socialized in a material world that tends to reduce everything to matter. What we do not readily see, we disregard as immaterial.

Our consciousness is inherent on all levels of our being. It is not isolated in any part of our being and is not restricted to our physical body. It is not restricted to your brain or your mind. Your brain operates your physical body. Your mind is a filter from your physical brain to your consciousness. Consciousness exists everywhere in creation in every aspect of life. It exists in nature and in all life forms. It exists in everything that is alive or aware on any level. Consciousness exists in every tree and also in every individual branch of a tree and every leaf of the tree. Consciousness permeates and propels all of life above and below, directing life and sustaining it, according to stanzas in *The Book of Dzyan*, the Tibetan mystic text considered to be the oldest manuscript in existence. Consciousness expands with growing awareness. And consciousness exists on every level of your being, on every extension of your being. That includes your subtle energy bodies outside your physical body. It is a nonphysical energy form that propels and sustains life with awareness. We communicate with awareness. Our consciousness with its awareness connects us with everything within us and outside us. If you want to open yourself to outside communication from unseen sources, I can offer you a very basic exercise for meditating to put yourself in the right state to become a ready receptor. Now, this could enable you to "hear" unseen voices from readily recognized sources too. You could become receptive to thought forms and telepathic messages from people and animals that you know. You could learn to listen to your houseplants and the trees around your house. You could listen to the birds around you and your pets. You could learn to become a good listener on many levels and become open to many outside messages that might come to you in nonverbal ways.

EXERCISE: MEDITATING TO OPEN YOURSELF TO OUTSIDE COMMUNICATION

NEEDED:

*A quiet, secluded room where you can safely meditate without interruption.
*A straight-back chair for you to use, or else a mat or blanket for you to recline on the ground.
*Loose-fitting clothing with shoes and all jewelry removed.

PROCEDURE:

Recline on your back with arms and legs outstretched to 45-degree angles, or sit erect in a straight-back chair with your feet firmly grounded, hands and arms open and not crossed, and your back very straight. Close your eyes and slowly put your body to sleep. Focus your attention on your feet and then your entire legs and tell them to become numb and go to sleep. Then focus your attention on your midsection and instruct this part of your body to become numb and go to sleep. Next, focus on your chest and arms and tell this section of your body to become numb and go to sleep. Then do the same with your head, until the very hairs on the top of your head have become numb and go to sleep. Begin deep, controlled breathing. Become conscious of the energizing quality of the air you take in, and count to three until your lungs are totally full. Hold the air inside you as you slowly count to three and sense the invigorating quality of this oxygen. Then slowly exhale this air to the count of three, consciously blessing the air and everything it touches when it leaves you. Continue this process until the rhythm becomes routine and you no longer need to consciously count and focus on what you are doing. Sustain this rhythmic, deep breathing through this exercise and all meditations. Tune out all external distractions and sensory input so that you hear nothing, feel nothing, and sense nothing outside you with your five senses. Next, tune out all internal chatter, so that you have no words or thoughts going through your mind. Forget about any thoughts about past things or concerns about the future. Stop all internal analysis. Allow your brain to relax and cease processing information, other than control of your routine bodily functions. Tell yourself that you are going to allow your body to relax and that you will be safe for the duration. Allow your brain to shut down to this degree. Picture a blank slate in front of your mind's eye. Focus your attention only on the blankness in front of you. You might see that as a blackboard or as a whiteboard. But you see nothing but the blankness. At this point, your superconsciousness should be engaged, as your consciousness raises to new heights of super-awareness. You are keenly aware, with your consciousness racing at a new level. Allow yourself to remain in this state, keenly alert and aware. You are in a listening mode. You are receptive. All of creation is around you and available for you to tap into. You are open to listen. Simply remain in this meditative state, with no thoughts or words internally. You are not distracted. You become a perfect witness. You are a perfect receiver. All information is available to you, if you allow yourself to listen. You can hear thoughts, ideas, and directed messages from unseen sources of the world known to you, and messages from beyond the world known to you. Be patient and wait. Timelessness is part of meditation. Things take as long to transpire as they require. When you sense that you have received something significant in your listening role, then you can slowly allow your focus to drift back to your physical body, allow sensation to return to your physical body, and then open your eyes. Allow yourself a time to adjust to returning to your physical body before attempting to stand. Review what you have learned and reflect deeply upon it. It might be useful to return to a meditative state to focus on what you have learned, with the intent to put that communication on the blank slate in front of your mind's eye for review.

5

YOU HAVE EARS AND YET YOU DO NOT HEAR

Great teachers and masters have long admonished their seekers to learn to listen better, hear better, and knock to open doors of understanding. You may be thinking that every healthy person has the ability to hear, listen, and ask questions, right? But great masters ask more of their students than idle listening and glancing eyes. They ask their students to reach beyond the five perceptive skills of the ordinary, physical world to have a deeper insight to universal intelligence.

"Having eyes, see ye not, and having ears, hear ye not?" Jesus Christ challenged his disciples in Mark 8:18 in the King James Version of the Holy Bible. He rebuked them for their lack of spiritual discernment.

Christ ended all seven letters to the church in Revelation with "He that hath an ear, let him hear," according to Matthew 13:9, referring to those who were "to know the mysteries of the kingdom of heaven" (Matthew 13:11).

Revelation 3:6 refers to ears to "hear what the Spirit saith." Hebrews 4:7 advises us to learn to "hear His voice."

But how can we become discerning and learn to discriminate as we seek to improve our hearing and hear the right messages from beyond? We can view discernment as perception and the ability to understand. Lack of discernment, by contrast, shows a lack of refinement, cultivation, sophistication, sensitivity, and enlightenment. Lack of discernment indicates an inability to discriminate from what is important and what is not.

Now, you are probably thinking that everyone with experience can listen carefully with their ears and see everything important around them with their eyes to discern what is important, right? But what if there is a deeper level of perception involved here, a level beyond the five perceptive senses of our ordinary, physical experience? Perhaps we are looking deeper for a heightened sense of awareness that goes beyond our five senses and the ordinary, physical world. After all, that is where masters usually direct us to seek deeper truth.

KRISHNAMURTI AND CASTAÑEDA

Indian sage Jiddu Krishnamurti, author of *At the Feet of the Master*, had much to say about developing discernment. "You as individuals have to comprehend the process of consciousness through direct, choiceless discernment," Krishnamurti said in Ommen, Holland, in 1936. "So, there must be deep, choiceless perception to comprehend the process of consciousness. If there is no discernment of the process of individual consciousness, then action will ever create confusion." He added that "this great discernment of choiceless life implies great alertness."

The Mexican American writer Carlos Castañeda wrote several books on developing a heightened sense of awareness by learning to see without eyes and to hear without ears, in what he described as "non-ordinary reality." His teachers encouraged him to open up on a deeper level of consciousness to see the unseen world all around us.

Lest anyone dismiss the books of Castañeda as fantasy or total fiction, consider that his first book was actually a project for his doctorate degree in anthropology from the University of California. I know this to be true, because I worked at a publishing house that reviewed his first book, *The Teachings of Don Juan: A Yaqui Way of Knowledge*. This excellent classic was based on field research with shamans in ancient Mexico. As a result, Carl Weschcke of Llewellyn Publications told me that he passed on this otherwise exciting manuscript on the grounds that it was clearly the thesis paper of a graduate student. This book and others by the young anthropologist described his shamanic training by Mexicans who traced their ancient Toltec roots in mysticism.

In book after book based on notes that Castañeda claimed he kept during his instruction, his mystic teachers encouraged him to see not with his eyes, but with a greater awareness and to learn to listen with a sense of heightened consciousness to a world outside our normal senses that most people do not hear or see for lack of training.

THE CHRISTIAN BIBLE

Concerns for this lack of seeing and hearing on a deeper level to reach inner, hidden truth are apparent through the Christian Bible. Biblical references to ears that do not hear and eyes that do not see precede even the recorded teachings of Jesus, with many such references found in the Old Testament. In Deuteronomy 29:4, it is written, "Yet the Lord hath not given you a heart to perceive, and eyes to see, and ears to hear unto this day."

In Jeremiah 5:21, it is written, "Hear now this, O foolish people, and without understanding; which have eyes, and see not; which have ears, and hear not."

Similarly, we see in Ezekiel 12:2: "Son of man, thou dwell in the midst of a rebellious house, which have eyes to see, and see not; they have ears to hear, and hear not."

Isaiah 42:18–20 says, "Hear, ye deaf; and look, ye blind, that ye may see. . . . Seeing many things, but thou observest not; opening the ears, but he heareth not." And Isaiah 44:18 continues this point: "They have not known nor understood: for he hath shut their eye, that they cannot see; and their hearts, that they cannot understand."

In Psalms 69:23, it says, "Let their eyes be darkened, that they see not." And in Psalms 115:5, it is written, "They have mouths, but they speak not; eyes have they, but they see not. They have ears, but they hear not."

The New Testament of the Bible contains many such references to deeper seeing and deeper listening. Mark 4:12 says, "That seeing they may see, and not perceive; and hearing they may hear, and not understand."

John 12:40 says, "He hath blinded their eyes, and hardened their hearts, that they should not see with their eyes." Apparently, people have been born half deaf and blind for many years.

In Romans 11:8, it is written, "God hath given them the spirit of slumber, eyes that they should not see, and ears that they should not hear."

A lot of us seem to be asleep and missing a lot of important things being said and otherwise communicated. Who is speaking to us? What are these unheard messages from beyond the pale? Likely, it could be divine voices, possibly the voice of God, angels, guides, nature spirits, or devas. It could be voices from the grave or other realms of the spirit world. It could be people you know who are desperately trying to reach you with information that they consider vital. It could be your lost pet. It could be voices from the past or the future. The possibilities are vast in a cosmos as large as ours, with worlds within worlds and endless skies before us. The question, always, is whether we are listening and attentive.

FOR THOSE WHO KNOCK

The young J. Krishnamurti dedicated his early classic, *At the Feet of the Master*, "to Those Who Knock." Indeed, the seeker needs to indicate a receptivity for knowledge, a desire to hear deeper truths that might be revealed to those who are ready. And as the Indian sage acknowledges in his little classic, the seeker might just as easily be Buddhist, Hindu, Muslim, Jew, Jain, or Christian. Truth is truth to whoever knocks on the door and listens in earnest.

"Knock, and it shall be opened unto you," reads Luke 11:5 in the King James Version of the Bible. "For everyone that asketh receiveth," it continues, "and he that seeketh findeth; and to him that knocketh it shall be opened."

Similarly, Matthew 7:7 of the King James Version of the Bible states: "Ask, and it shall be given you; seek, and yet shall find; knock, and it shall be opened unto you."

It sounds like good advice, divine guidance. And it's certainly good communication skills. The basic thing we must do to receive communication is to make ourselves available by listening, reaching a level of conscious awareness, and acknowledging that we are ready to hear what special messages might be directed to us. And part of that is learning to knock on the door to acknowledge our presence and willingness to receive guests with something to impart.

This is not to say that we are trying to establish contact, but only that we are present and receptive. Knocking on the door need not initiate communication; it could signal our receptivity. Having said that, it's important to impart some possible precautions here. This book does not in any way advocate summoning the dead, invoking unseen spirits, or any other sort of high magic and mediumship that seeks to open communication. That can be dangerous and is probably unethical.

PRECAUTIONS

This precaution comes from two of my favorite teachers—Madam Helena P. Blavatsky, noted clairvoyant and author of *The Secret Doctrine*, and psychic author Louis Gittner, my first teacher.

Blavatsky apparently was interested during her early life in developing psychic abilities and forming a group to study clairvoyant abilities. She had a very interesting relationship with adept masters of the Himalayans, the so-called mahatmas, who trained her at their mountain retreat and then would contact her to assist with her occult writing and her failing health. They apparently wouldn't travel physically to contact her but would sort of drop in on her, materializing for a brief time to communicate or dropping off helpful letters that fell from the sky.

The key point here is that she did not always initiate these mysterious contacts from the adept masters but was receptive to their mystic visits. Also, Blavatsky denounced mediumship when she began to report what she had learned from the mahatmas and founded the international Theosophical Society to study their views on cosmology and what they outlined to her as the divine plan of spiritual evolution. She discouraged so-called table tipping or séances. She encouraged seekers to open themselves up as spiritual vessels.

Similarly, Louis Gittner as a spiritual teacher discouraged me and other students from trying to contact the spirit realm or unseen voices, because he saw the practice as unreliable and possibly dangerous. He taught me that a person who tries to initiate contact with the spirit realm could not reliably predict who would answer or that the contact would be exactly as described to you.

ADVICE FROM A GHOST HUNTER

As a former ghost hunter who was trained as a student of Louis Gittner to assist ghosts in moving on by making contact, I can assure you that this precaution about initiating contact with the spirit realm is very practical and wise to follow. I would go into a house that was deemed to be haunted by a restless spirit, and try to make contact. People who call you into their home situations to resolve problems with restless spirits generally figure that it's their mother, son, or other close family member who once lived with them years ago. Or maybe they figure that the spirit who haunted their home was a former resident before their family moved there.

Often the truth proves daunting, at least on the basis of my experience and stories that I have heard from other ghost hunters. Spirits may seek to deceive you if you initiate contact and welcome them into your life. They might present themselves as your maiden aunt or a former resident but turn out to be something quite different. There is just no telling at the outset.

If you encounter a deceptive spirit, you might find yourself dealing with a trickster, a malevolent spirit, or a dark entity that seeks only to torment and manipulate you. They can plant thought form impressions of who they are and what they might look like, but those might turn out to be only illusions projected to you. And once you summon them and initiate contact, you cannot always get rid of them.

My earlier book *Confessions of a Reluctant Ghost Hunter* relates some of my communication attempts gone wrong. There is a reason why we gave this book the subtitle *A Cautionary Tale of Encounters with Malevolent Entities and Other Disembodied Spirits*.

On one occasion, I was asked to make contact with a spirit in a mobile home in the middle of the woods on Mount Hood in Oregon, where a girl who lived there described playing with a spirit girl with curly blonde hair, and the parents in the home described an invisible spirit that tried to shock them in their sleep. When I finally contacted the entity, it turned out to be not a little girl with blonde curls, but a hideous creature who preyed on anything that occupied that section of the forest. The site had been occupied earlier and suddenly abandoned. Names of deceased pets were carved into a tree. When I tried to convince this entity to leave, it refused and attacked me. Later, the mobile home caught fire mysteriously and the family's dog died in the fire, tied under the dwelling.

I suspect that this entity still haunts these woods, assuming whatever disguise seems likely to work on people it encounters. For that reason, I have never returned there. Some things are best left alone. Some things should stay corked in a bottle and ignored. It might prove difficult to return them to the bottle once it's opened.

My recommendation as a retired ghost hunter these days is to allow your deceased father, pet, or favorite aunt to visit you and make contact on their own, and not to initiate the contact yourself. Sometimes the deceased will spend a few days making the rounds to say goodbye and take a last look around before leaving. But then most deceased people move on.

Blavatsky was clear on the need to allow spirits of our deceased loved ones to move on to evolve spiritually and continue with the next phase of their lives. She said that it was unkind to try to drag them into conversations back here once they were ready to move on. All life needs to evolve. For that reason, she spoke against mediums and séances.

If a deceased loved one chooses to contact you, as they might likely do shortly after physical death, then be open to listening. But do not seek to contact them. And when you receive a spirit communication, try to listen with your heart. If the contact that comes to you feels right to your heart and resonates with your every fiber of being and with your inner soul being, then it is probably a safe source.

UNION WITH THE DIVINE

Krishnamurti encouraged union with the divine, a primary goal for serious study of yoga. He described love in *At the Feet of the Master* as an intense desire for liberation from the rounds of birth and death "and for union with God." It is, he said, the desire to be one with God. The divine spark within you should resonate when you are in union with God. So if an entity seeks to communicate with you and you do not resonate in that way on a deep, spiritual level, then that entity probably should be avoided, regardless of how it might represent itself.

Louis Gittner once assisted me with unwelcomed messages sent to me by dark figures in the night. These were troublesome contacts aimed at me by suspicious people who were sending me telepathic messages from a remote part of Mount Hood when I lived there. Their psychic attacks were unwelcomed and troublesome to my guests as well. They would materialize briefly in a sort of astral body in the skylight over my double A-frame house, as I learned when reclining on my back in the living room there one day at dusk. A few days later, someone else saw them hovering over my skylight, looking down into my mountain home. I asked Louis how to send them packing, as a message that I did not want to receive.

He told me to meditate on the purest love that I could imagine and then project that love toward them. The idea, apparently, was that the love would transform them or else clash with them and their intent, gumming things up. It worked. I sent ribbons of pure love to them and never heard from them again.

I think of that now as a cosmic rubber band that will either connect you and the other party in loving harmony or snap in their face. Either way, it seems like a safe and pure way to refuse a message with no karmic consequences. How they deal with the love that you send is totally up to them.

Louis Gittner always told me that you could tell immediately in this way if you were contacted by a loving, divine spirit, as he was by the nature spirits. They would sweep across him and through his body with a wave of joy, love, and peace. He would smile upon hearing from them. He could sense a good incoming message and messenger from a bad one. But he reminded me, too, that he was very psychic and experienced in spirit communication. Obviously, practice here is essential. Toward that end, we will attempt here to outline how to establish safe and secure lines of communication with the unseen world. Mysterious messages from beyond need not be frightening or harmful.

6

OUR THOUGHTS
HAVE POWER

What we learn to hear when we develop "new ears" will likely be nonauditory sound or simply powerful thoughts being broadcast in our direction. Words without sound are thought forms that are conveyed by consciousness and received by consciousness. No ears in the physical sense will be required. This is what Carlos Castañeda liked to call *nonordinary reality*. It's as real as any Mozart symphony, however, or any great and moving speech that we might hear—but without sound. That is why mysterious messages from beyond often are heard by only a small number of people. The recipients of these messages must have acute listening skills, attuned through the development of heightened states of consciousness.

Let us examine for a moment the power of thought forms. Let's look at some controlled studies that involve a large number of people who have learned to communicate without sound. The Beatles helped popularize an Indian guru, the Maharishi Mahesh Yogi, whom they encouraged to bring his form of deep meditation to the West. He was the student of an Indian master from the Himalayas and eager to teach deep meditation, which was called Transcendental Meditation (TM). The maharishi predicted in 1960 that only 1 percent of the population engaged in his TM technique of deep meditation could improve life quality for the entire population. This was tested in the early '70s and reported in a study published in 1976. The conclusion of the study was that when 1 percent of a community practiced this TM technique, the crime rate was reduced by approximately 16 percent. This phenomenon has been termed the Maharishi effect and has been replicated worldwide.

Many of you have probably observed this on a personal level with group prayer or sending healing thoughts to someone whom your entire group held dear. When we sing a song together, people are moved. When we chant or recite together, as with a pledge, it seems to move people deeply. Group thought has great power.

Let us look at the impact of the maharishi and the Maharishi effect through the years. Since the study of the TM technique of group meditation, more than four dozen studies have sought to replicate the effect. Most studies suggest that the power of group meditation can transform global lifestyle patterns. A similar TM study in Wales produced very positive results. Merseyside had one of the highest crime rates among eleven of the largest metropolitan centers in England, but by 1992 it had the lowest crime rate. In fact, Merseyside reported 225,000 fewer crimes from 1988 to 1992.

Maharishi Mahesh Yogi's 1963 book on the TM technique, *Science of Being and Art of Living*, is still the best introduction to the practice and has sold more than a million copies in the United States alone, in addition to countless other copies in other editions worldwide. Serious use of deep meditation by a dedicated group could probably stop war and terrorism worldwide on a permanent basis, according to Dr. John Hagelin's summary of more than fifty studies conducted with the TM technique. The ancient sages, according to Dr. Hagelin, were correct about the peace-creating power of human consciousness. He points out that sciences of our age have combined with ageless wisdom today to create a practical, powerful technology of peace. Ageless knowledge of the power of consciousness is what is behind the meditation technique of the maharishi's teachings, according to Dr. Hagelin of the international group's institute. These teachings have evolved from the ancient Vedic tradition in the Hinduism of India. The Vedic scriptures generally predate Hinduism and contain the insight of various early sages without any particular religious orientation. The sacred texts became a part of Hinduism. The Vedic tradition, so important to a serious study of deep meditation and thought power today, considers the role of consciousness. The tradition emphasizes a subjective view of unmanifest consciousness and the basic reality of both the individual and the cosmos in the process of meditation. Vedic meditation techniques seek the direct experience and awareness of the unmanifest-consciousness field.

The Vedic tradition is 5,000 years old and is often considered the oldest continuous tradition of knowledge on Earth. Today, meditation in a state of heightened consciousness is practiced by many people of various traditions around the world. Meditation is practiced by Hindus, Buddhists, and many others. One might make an argument that serious, deep prayer is actually a form of meditation, just as sending healing or loving thoughts to others is a form of meditation. If we consider the thought power of 1 percent throughout the world, consider the impact of even ten meditators in any given community when collectively focused in deep group meditation. Our thoughts have form and impact, according to the early writings of occultists Annie Besant and C. W. Leadbeater, early Theosophists steeped in Eastern spiritual science. Our thoughts when focused and aimed efficiently in deep meditation can reach target audiences with accuracy and even move mountains, as conscious energy that has form and power.

THOUGHT FORMS AND THOUGHT POWER

For the purpose of this discussion about meditating to form thoughts, we will consider the works of Annie Besant and Charles Leadbeater (*Thought Forms and Thought Power* and *The Yoga Sutras of Patanjali*). Besant and Leadbeater, two early clairvoyant authors, examined the actual form of thoughts as they left persons, and where these thought forms had an impact and with what effect. When we refer to our consciousness in the context of meditations and forming thought forms, we are referring to higher consciousness or a level of conscious thought that is above the normal functioning of our physical brain, and probably above what many people commonly call our mind. Our higher consciousness is connected to our higher self or spirit and can exist outside our body and outside space and time. It is what takes you on your out-of-body travel in vivid, lucid dreaming. It is where you see yourself when you have precognition visions of yourself in the future, or flashbacks of where you were in past lives. It's what you will take with you when you transition beyond the physical plane in mortal death and enter the pure energy world of spirit. So, I really like to think of our higher consciousness as conscious awareness, an insightful awareness of the inner spirit that transcends our five physical senses and limited sense of three dimensions in a linear, mundane world.

Clairvoyants such as Besant and Leadbeater have been able to document the look of thought forms projected out of our consciousness. Most people, even today, consider thoughts just to be empty ideas inside a person's head that do not leave the person except when verbalized. They see no shape or color to the thoughts as forms. They see them as empty wishes or ideas without impact. The classic text *Thought Forms* by Besant and Leadbeater assigns observed colors with various vibrational levels to thoughts that cover a wide spectrum. They observe runaway thoughts of anger, avarice, malice, and selfishness that come with raw emotional energy on the part of the sender. They see malice as black, anger as bold red, and avarice as a pinker red. They also see random thoughts of sensuality as crimson and selfishness as dark green. They see thought forms of depression as dark brown with spots, and jealousy as gray and red streaks. They see fear as purple and deceit as gray.

Runaway thoughts that cut recklessly outward in any which direction come out of our human consciousness. There is consciousness in all of creation—consciousness in the source of all life, consciousness in nature, and consciousness in people as well, according to Blavatsky's "First Fundamental Proposition," which is based on her teaching from the mahatmas on the *Stanzas of Dzyan*. The consciousness that drives our emotional outbursts in thoughts is filled with desire. Little if any mental energy, however, comes from our lower self and lower consciousness as opposed to our higher consciousness. Our higher consciousness is energized by our mental body, our creative causal body, and our higher spiritual bodies that bring us to self-realization, cosmic consciousness, and our divine connection. Thoughts that emerge with focus and greater awareness from our higher consciousness come from our spiritual self with a grander purpose and understanding of our connection to the oneness in all. Our higher consciousness comes out of our spiritual connection with all life, with an ability to innately understand the interrelationship and interdependence of all life as sacred and precious. Higher consciousness can be accessed through meditation that is either deliberate and active or part of a way of life whereby we live our lives meditatively.

When we focus our higher consciousness, we can direct regulated thought forms carefully to intended targets with better effect. There is mental, spiritual, or causal energy of a higher nature behind this energy, and not just raw emotional energy. That is the sort of focused consciousness that you will find in the meditations outline for the advanced yoga student in *The Yoga Sutras*.

Focused thought forms from a higher level of consciousness, Leadbeater and Besant observed, assume the colors most closely associated with the powerful chakras or energy centers in the body. Mental energy sends the highest intellect in bright yellow created out of the mental plane. Pure affection will assume a pinkish red, emitted by the root chakra. Thought forms of high spirituality will appear as a royal blue with light flecks, while devotion to a noble cause may appear as an even-deeper, solid blue. Religious devotion could appear almost purple. Sympathy that we send to someone, the clairvoyant authors said, could appear as a light green. Love for humanity could appear as soft pink, while unselfish affection would likely appear darker pink, and pure affection an even-darker, bolder pink. Clearly, then, our thought forms are laced with colors associated with energy. That energy that powers our thought forms can be from physical energy, emotional energy, mental energy, causal energy, or spiritual energy. These colors have different properties and have different impact upon arrival. When we learn to control the light that we absorb and intensify within us in our thought power, we realize our true human potential as light vessels and light bringers. Angels are pure beings of life that radiate effulgent light and bring light wherever they go. They are pure light beings. We are human light vessels who must learn to become a part of cocreation on the level of development we occupy on the earth training grounds we inhabit. It is a tremendous challenge and opportunity—the greatest that any of us will ever realize in this human existence. We are supremely blessed with the amazing opportunity to develop as light bringers.

Consider each one of us, therefore, a great hero on a journey of discovery. The true hero finds not only the path that leads somewhere to something, which is almost anticlimactic in the grand picture. True heroes on an adventure of discovery will find something in themselves or about themselves. Along the way, they discover themselves and insightful hidden truths about themselves that were not known at the outset. That is the arc of the true hero's journey—the point at which they discover something unforeseen about themselves and the human condition.

Life, after all, is a grand adventure of discovery. If you are here to simply enjoy yourself and avoid getting dirty or exhausted, you have missed the point. Your life is a proving ground for you to start your journey on a path of discovery and growth. When you have grown and become a true light bringer, you will become infinitely more valuable in the grand scheme of things as a cocreator in this universe. The universe, you see, is hardly complete, but in a process of becoming, much like ourselves. You are needed. Your creative thoughts are needed to form and create. And they require refinement. We are complex creatures at this point—physical, emotional, mental, creative, intuitive, self-aware, outwardly observant, and spiritually motivated. Indeed, we are a combination of all these aspects of our many subtle bodies and the energy vortexes that drive them. We are connected to many planes of reality and existence. As a result, our thoughts blur with various energy and the colors associated with these colors. Gifted aura readers will note how colors leave our outer shells in blended combinations. You will not see all one color distinctly, but a combination of combinations that contribute to our thought forms leaving our body either intentionally or with focus awareness. Our desire is a complex thing that can combine emotional energy sometimes seen as reddish light with orange light that comes more from our higher desire in the creative center of our causal body. Or you might see the causal body emitting orange light energy swirled and blended with soft yellow light from the mental plane in a combination of desire and mental energy.

With focused intent, we can learn to package the energy that drives our thoughts in creative visualization with the sort of light properties that affect meaningful change. The challenge to that is to learn to picture what we want to do and how we can best engineer it. Creative visualization at its core is really effectively engineering our imagination and driving it with a picture of what we want to achieve, laced with the power to make it happen. The power behind your thought forms does not simply drive the thoughts to their targets but empowers the change from taking place on impact. You need the right currency to ride each different bus you want to take. The right currency, in this case, is the sort of light energy you need to effect change. Always remember that each color of light has different properties and corresponds to different planes of existence.

It was previously thought by pioneers in thought forms, such as Besant and Leadbeater, that the energy vibrations in our focused thought transference were strongest and tightest as waves closest to the sender. That leads one to believe that there is a range of effect thought transference, which actually does seem to favor being close to the subject you want to send thought forms or affect with creative visualization. If you experiment with sending thought forms, you will probably discover that it's usually easier with the target in the room or when there are numerous senders of the same message. The vibrations are strongest then. But we know now that the vibrations continue for some distance. You have probably at some time picked up on someone sending you thought forms. Another mammal, the whale, is known to send messages to others around the world across an entire ocean or even from one ocean to another. Thoughts not only have form, but they have power.

Clairvoyants Besant and Leadbeater were guided in their study of thought forms and thought power by a study of classic Eastern spiritual science and primarily *The Yoga Sutras of Pantanjali*. This classic book really taught the world how to meditate with effectiveness. It is a serious study of yoga that divides meditation into various levels, including transformation or magic and mysticism. It studies various states of heightened consciousness that the serious student of yoga can approach in meditation. You can begin to study inaudible messages from beyond that are transferred telepathically or by thought power by studying this textbook of meditation practices.

GEOFFREY HODSON ON THOUGHT FORMS

Our projected thoughts leave our sender's body as vibrating waves. Another clairvoyant author, Geoffrey Hodson, saw two immediate effects produced by strong, concentrated thought waves. Hodson, a minister, described the visual effects of thought waves in his book *Basic Theosophy*. The first immediate effect, according to the New Zealander, was radiating vibrations that occur in the thinker's mental body and then transfer to the surrounding mental atmosphere. Hodson said that was similar to the way the vibration of a bell is transferred to the surrounding air.

The second immediate effect, Hodson said, was the actual formation of thought forms. In the case of a mental impulse, the radiation is not in one plane of our complex being only, but in many dimensions, akin to the radiation cast by a lamp. Whenever thought waves encounter another mental body, they tend to set up vibrations similar to those of the incident vibrations. It appears, Hodson reasoned, that the most important factor in the interaction between mental bodies is not so much of the strength, but the clarity and definition of the original thought.

Emotional thoughts that affect the astral body are usually deflected or overwhelmed by a multitude of other vibrations at the same level and therefore do not generally affect others, according to *Theosopedia*. A notable exception is seen in large crowds that are astrally stimulated by a shared emotional experience. We can see that happening at a sporting event where people share an emotional experience. So, we can determine that thought power of a group of people is greater than the sum of their individual thoughts.

SYBIL LEEK AND IAN FLEMING

So what do the white witch Sybil Leek and the creator of James Bond have to do with this discussion? Because they meditated together for many years during World War II to bring about peace. This was a little bit before the Beatles found the maharishi and brought him to the West. But like the maharishi, Sybil Leek and Ian Fleming engaged in deep group meditation to end the war and bring peace to the world. This was only a few people meditating together to bring thoughts of peace into reality in the world around them, far less than 1 percent of the world's population. So, consider the power of two.

We must consider the likelihood, of course, that more than just these few people were meditating on peace at the time. Around the world, many people were undoubtedly sending these thought forms in a state of heightened consciousness. The fact that they were not gathered in one room makes it hard to measure, but their collective consciousness nonetheless had impact on a group scale.

MADAME HELENA P. BLAVATSKY

H. P. Blavatsky in her *Collected Writings* introduced a term for consciousness and thought forms called *nolens volens*. "Every thought so evolved with energy from the brain creates a nolens volens (willing) shape," she wrote. Such a shape is absolutely unconscious unless the sender has a preconceived object in giving this particular thought form consciousness or the appearance of consciousness. That comes from the sender's will and consciousness. So, we see the importance of exercising our will at a deep level of our being when we focus our consciousness and project our thought forms.

HIDDEN MESSAGES IN WATER

We cannot discuss group thought form projection without including the modern research of the amazing Japanese researcher Masaru Emoto. In Emoto's experiments in *The Hidden Messages in Water*, a group of people were asked to focus their shared thought and emotional attention on one worthy subject. Emoto's subject group could collectively transform the crystal structure of water and send loving, healing thoughts to a common target. He worked with young children to send loving, healing thoughts as a group, with equally amazing results.

Emoto appeared in some amazing videos to describe his work. His experiments in effective use of thought power were replicated by others throughout the world. Thought forms can have long-term effects, too, and have a lasting effect on other people. Thought forms can attach themselves to the object of the thoughts and generate results that can be very beneficial, but also potentially harmful. Strongly focused thought over a period of time can change the atmosphere in the environment around us as well as objects, for good or ill. Negative thought forms, if they remain, can be detrimental to the thinker who projects them. Conversely, positive thoughts that generate corresponding thought forms can result in a positive reinforcement for the thinker.

Thought forms that migrate to their target can rebound if the recipient's mental aura is a different level of subtle mental energy. On the other hand, if the nature of thought form and the mental aura of the target are in perfect harmony, then the thought form could be absorbed, improving or reinforcing the condition of the recipient. This accounts for effectiveness of long-distance healing performed by gifted healers such as Edgar Cayce.

7

EXPLORING
VOICELESS MESSAGES

We have been exploring how it is possible for people to receive mysterious messages that are not audible but nonetheless connect with them on a personal level. Now we will explore how exercises allow you to experience nonverbal communication that require no voices or ears to be effective. This involves thought transference or thought power. Sometimes it is called telepathic communication, a description that tends to give it an occult connotation. Let us remember, however, that occult really means hidden, secret, or not physically measurable. Occult studies are a look into the unseen world. Just because something is not as obvious as something that you can see with your eyes or hear with your ears does not mean that it doesn't exist. That limits our reality to our five physical senses and a limited, material view of everything around us. It is a simplistic and limited way of reducing our connection to reality to a material sense of what we can physically put our hands on.

So, the following exercises will introduce you, on a very personal level, to thought forms and telepathy as an individual who sends or receives voiceless communication as part of a group that projects thought forms and as a person who receives group thought forms. By the end of these exercises, you should be convinced that anyone can learn to send and receive telepathic communication with a little practice and heightened focus.

Our first exercise will give you some practice sending a thought form to another person in an adjoining room. Then we will ask you to switch roles with the person in the other room to receive a message from the other person.

EXERCISE: RECEIVING MYSTERIOUS MESSAGES
FROM BEYOND

NEEDED:

*Two adjacent rooms separated by a door, with no visibility between the two rooms. Both rooms should be quiet and secluded, without outside interference.
*A straight-back chair or a mat in both rooms. You could substitute a blanket or pad in place of a mat.
*Two people, one in each room, both wearing loose-fitting clothes with shoes and jewelry removed

PROCEDURE:

In this first exercise, you will assume the role of message sender and attempt to telepathically communicate with the person in the other room. There should be no clue between the two parties of any sort for this to work. The message to be sent is a secret known only to the one person who will send the message.

Both of you should recline on a floor mat, faceup, with arms and legs extended to a 45-degree angle, or else sit erect in a straight-back chair with shoeless feet firmly planted on the ground. Both of you should close your eyes and allow your physical body to become numb. Tell your legs to relax and go to sleep. Then tell your midsection to relax and become numb as well. Then focus your attention on your upper body and tell it to relax and go to sleep. Finally, focus on your chin, nose, cheeks, and ears and the top of your head in telling the rest of your body to relax and go to sleep. Assure your brain that it can relax, too, and rest for a while during a short meditation.

Begin and continue rhythmic, deep breathing. Both parties should reach a still point deep within themselves, tuning out all recognition of outside sounds and other distractions and tuning out all internal dialogue. Both of you should clear the inner mind until all around you is still and quiet and you are staring at a blank screen before your mind's eye deep inside you. As the person who is designated to send the secret message, you should visualize the person to receive the message in the other room. See the image or impression of this person's face. Now project the message that you want to send to that person. Visualize the message. Try not to use words or sentences. Instead, construct the message as an image or a picture. Convey the meaning, not the words. If you form words and construct sentences, you tend to employ your analytical brain.

Once the person in the other room feels that the message has been received, that person should come into the other room to confer with you about the message as received. It might be that the message was only partly received or received in a slightly altered fashion. The two of you should discuss the message that was sent, and the message as received. Remember, practice makes perfect. You will get better at sending thought form messages the more you work at it and focus your heightened consciousness in the process.

SWITCH ROLES

After doing this exercise the first time, you should switch roles, so that you are now the receiver and the other person has the role of message sender. Once again, wear loose-fitting clothing without shoes or jewelry and sit on straight-back chairs or recline faceup on mats, as before. You should change rooms, so that you are now in the room first occupied by the other participant and that person is in the room you first occupied. Do not confer or prompt each other in any way. The message that the other party will attempt to send to you now should be a secret.

Begin and continue deep, rhythmic breathing. Take some time to focus on putting your bodies to sleep again, starting with your legs and working your attention to the top of your head. Then reassure your brain to relax as well, allowing it to rest during your meditation with the assurance that you will be physically safe and well rested during this short period.

Tune out all external distractions and clear your inner mind, reaching a still point deep within you where you see only a blank slate in your mind's eye. The other party will now visualize you and then project the message to be sent to you in the other room. Take your time, staying focused in a state of heightened consciousness. When you feel that you have received the message, join the other person in the next room to confer. See how close you came to receiving the full message intact. Don't be discouraged if you were only partially successful or had trouble receiving the message. You can always try again and work to perfect your communication skills.

NOTE: The preceding exercise should assure you that mysterious messages from beyond can reach you in private communications. They can reach you without a sound or anyone in sight, oblivious to anyone but you. Next, we will

give you a chance to personally experience receiving a group message and sending a message as part of a group who sends a telepathic message. You should notice more power and impact with a group involved in thought transfer.

EXERCISE: GROUP THOUGHT TRANSFER

NEEDED:

*Two adjacent rooms separated by a door. with no visibility between the two rooms. Both rooms should be quiet and secluded. without outside interference.
*A straight-back chair or a mat in both rooms (you could use a blanket or pad instead of a mat)
*A group of at least three people in one room as message senders, and a single person

in the other room to receive the message that they will project using thought power
*In this exercise, I suggest that you include yourself in the group who sends the message. Later you can switch sides and experience receiving the message from the group who sends it.

*A simple, mutually agreed-on message that the group will send. Write down the message once you agree on it, so that everyone in the group has a copy to study and memorize. This should be done with the other person who will act as receiver in the other room, so they do not hear or see the message. Ideally, the group would do it as soon as the other person goes into the adjacent room to await their message.

Before you begin to approach getting into a meditative state to project the message, the group might want to recite the message a few times in unison to help implant it carefully in their memory, although it should be done quietly so the person in the other room cannot hear them. This recitation could be done with the group members in a circle close together.

PROCEDURE:

Both the person awaiting the message in the other room and the group who will send the message should sit erect in straight-back chairs, with shoeless feet firmly anchored on the ground, or reclined on the mat faceup with arms and legs all at 45-degree angles.

All participants should focus on putting their physical bodies to rest and tuning out all external distractions and all internal dialogue. All participants should begin and continue deep, rhythmic breathing. All participants should reach a still point deep inside them and focus on a clear, blank slate in their mind's eye.

The group who will send the message should visualize the person to whom they intend to send their message. They should remain quiet and nonverbal. Then the sending group should visualize the message that they all intend to send, without forming words or sentences inside them. Simply visualize the message superimposed over the image of the intended recipient. When the person in the other room feels that the message has been received, all participants should gather to discuss how accurately the message came through.

Open discussion might reveal whether variations in the received message involved variations in the way some of the people in the sending group remembered the message and projected it. It would be helpful to experience both sides of this communication exercise, so that you fully appreciate the process and realize how mysterious messages from beyond can reach us with particular impact when the message involves groups and not simply one-to-one personal contact.

SWITCH ROLES

After doing this exercise the first time, you should switch roles, so that you are now the receiver and the other people send you a message from the other room. The group who will send the message to you should agree on a message, and each should write down a copy of the message to study and memorize. Then they might gather in a small circle and quietly recite the message in unison three times before assuming their individual chairs or floor positions to put themselves in a state of heightened consciousness to project the message.

Once again, wear loose-fitting clothing without shoes or jewelry, and sit on straight-back chairs or recline faceup on mats, as before. You should change rooms, so that you are now in the room first occupied by the other participant and that person is in the room you first occupied. Do not confer or prompt each other in any way. The message that the other party will attempt to send to you now should be a secret.

Begin and continue deep, rhythmic breathing. Take some time to focus on putting your bodies to sleep again, starting with your legs and working your attention to the top of your head. Then reassure your brain to relax as well, allowing it to rest during your meditation with the assurance that you will be physically safe and well rested during this short period.

Tune out all external distractions and clear your inner mind, reaching a still point deep within you where you see only a blank slate in your mind. The messengers who are assembled as a group in the adjacent room will now visualize you and then project the message to be sent to you in the other room. Take your time, staying focused in a state of heightened consciousness.

When you feel that you have received the message, join the group in the next room to confer. See how close you came to receiving the full message intact. Do not be discouraged if you were only partially successful or had trouble receiving the message. You can always try again and work to perfect your communication skills.

We will now try the experiment in thought transfer with you as the sole communicator who sends your message to a group of people simultaneously. Consider the same message that my teacher Louis Gittner and the amazing gardeners at Findhorn received at precisely the same time. It would appear that the nature spirits who communicated with the Findhorn community were the same energy that communicated to Louis on Orcas Island in the San Juans.

EXERCISE: A SINGLE COMMUNICATOR WITH A SINGLE MESSAGE TO THE MASSES

NEEDED:

*Two adjacent rooms separated by a door, with no visibility between the two rooms
* Both rooms should be quiet and secluded, without outside interference.
* A straight-back chair or a mat in both rooms (you could use a blanket or pad instead of a mat)
* A group of at least three people in one room as participants who will receive the message, and you alone in the other room to project the message that they will receive.
* Determine on your own a secret message that you will send to the people in the other room. Make the message simple and study it to memorize it. You might consider writing it down to read over and over to implant it in your memory. Take care to provide no clues to the participants who will act as receivers. This should be done privately so the others who will act as receivers in the other room do not hear or see the message.

PROCEDURE:

Both you and the group who are awaiting the message in the other room should sit erect in straight-back chairs, with shoeless feet firmly anchored on the ground, or reclining on the mat faceup with arms and legs all at 45-degree angles.

All participants should focus on putting their physical bodies to rest and tuning out all external distractions and all internal dialogue. All participants should begin and continue deep, rhythmic breath. All participants should reach a still point deep inside them and focus on a clear, blank slate in their mind's eye. As the sender, you should visualize the persons to whom you intend to send this message. You should remain quiet and nonverbal.

Then you should visualize the message you intend to send, without forming words or sentences. Simply visualize the message superimposed over the image of the intended recipients. When the people in the other room feel that the message has been received, then all participants should gather to discuss how accurately the message came through.

VARIATION

This variation to the preceding exercise places all the participants who receive the message in different rooms instead of being assembled in the same room. The intent of this new exercise is to show you as the sender of the message that your message can be broadcast to various locations simultaneously. This is not as dramatic as having you send a telepathic message to someone in Scotland and someone else in the San Juan Islands, but it's a little more practical for our study and easier to arrange. If you find easy success in this test, you might want to try remote locations for another exercise, if you are able to coordinate participants.

NEEDED:

*Locate two or three participants in separate, nearby rooms where they will be from your own separate room.
*As before, all participants should select straight-back chairs for sitting or floor mats to recline faceup.
* All participants should wear loose clothing with shoes and jewelry removed.

PROCEDURE:

Both you and the participants who are awaiting the message in the other rooms should sit erect in straight-back chairs, with shoeless feet firmly anchored on the ground, or reclining on the mat faceup with arms and legs all at 45-degree angles.

All participants should focus on putting their physical bodies to rest and tuning out all external distractions and all internal dialogue. All participants should begin and continue deep, rhythmic breathing. All participants should reach a still point deep inside them and focus on a clear, blank slate with their mind's eye.

As the sender, you should visualize the persons to whom you intend to send this message. You should remain quiet and nonverbal. Then, visualize the message you intend to send without forming words or sentences. Simply visualize the message superimposed over the image of the intended recipients. When the people in the other rooms feel that the message has been received, then all participants should gather outside your door until all of them are ready to meet with you to discuss how accurately the message came through.

NOTE: When we first learned to communicate, we practiced by standing face to face with words and body language to make our messages clear. That is how we physically communicate with verbalization and facial expressions. Along the way, people seem to learn how to communicate without words, too, but with mixed results, due to lack of focus and practice. We think intently about someone and our thoughts fly from us, sometimes reaching the mark and sometimes scattering in all directions without much focus. I hope that the above exercises will give you some idea how thoughts can be transferred efficiently with focus and intent with a little practice. One hopes, too, that these exercises have convinced you of the likelihood that mysterious messages from beyond can reach you from almost any direction, if you are open to them and learn to listen.

8

THOUGHTS AS ENERGY ROLL FORTH LIKE WAVES

We need to think of our thoughts as energy waves sent forth by our consciousness. Our thought forms have power and impact, particularly if directed with intent and focus to reach a designated target. Consider the electromagnetic-field theory of radiant energy that is so integral to the groundbreaking work of geniuses in science from Michael Faraday to James Clerk Maxwell, Hendrik Lorentz, Oliver Heaviside, and Albert Einstein, among others. Electromagnetic energy radiates from the sun to energize all life, including the highly charged life force that runs throughout human bodies on all levels. Nothing that can be measured in our physical world seems to travel faster than the speed of light, if we can trust the celebrated work of Einstein, who tied the speed of light to how we experience subjectively where we stand. Light flows forth in wave action until it reaches its target.

We cannot discuss Einstein and his view on time-space, however, without considering another influence on Einstein as a visionary. In a sense, Einstein was a student of H. P. Blavatsky's occult study of the cosmos, *The Secret Doctrine*, and heavily wrote in the margins of his personal copy before his death, donating that book to the international Theosophical Society, a group founded by the psychic author H. P. Blavatsky.

She described a description in the very ancient Senzar language, believed to be the pictograph language of angels. It describes origins and operation of the cosmos and our place in it, which she discovered in study with adept masters in a Himalayan monastery. In *The Secret Doctrine*, she describes the universality and importance of consciousness behind all life.

Madame Blavatsky, a sort of go-between for ancient roots of Eastern spirit science with its arcane mysteries and our modern Western science, described a universal force that drives and sustains all of life from atom to cosmos. She said that universal consciousness is ever evolving and apparent above and below the grand design of creation, obvious in the changing cycles of creation and nature in our physical world. It is found in all life, including our own.

I submit that when we speak about universal consciousness, electromagnetic radiant energy, the seven recognized rays, and light in extension, we are speaking about a universal reality that cannot be denied. The evidence is all around us in the sun that powers all of life, intelligent design in all of life, and the spectrum of light in every rainbow. We are infused by this life force. We are light beings encased in physical matter to function physically in a physical world. We absorb, process, and transform light energy that we can project.

Of course, light, consciousness, and our life force cannot be so easily measured as nonphysical energy in a physical world. Not even Antoine-Laurent Lavoisier, the French father of chemistry, could measure the nonphysical with all of his precision, except to say that there is a gap between the world of physical matter and the nonphysical that could not be easily bridged in our world of weights and measures.

Exactly how we project the energy that runs through our body is most easily measured by impact of thought projection, the subject of this book. What is unseen and can't be physically measured in a material way can otherwise be measured by effect, right? So let's look at the thoughts that we project by their effect and impact on delivery.

To do this, we need to examine wave action. Just as water on an ocean or pond rolls outward in ripples, energy rolls like waves. Science certainly understands this principle and measures vibrational waves of physical sound. Light also is measured as vibrational waves that roll forward. If we think of our conscious thoughts as energy similar to light or sound, then it helps to think of wave action to track our thoughts spreading outward from us. As a fundamental principle, that would be true, then, of all conscious thoughts that are projected by any conscious life forms. Waves roll forward, impacting anything and everything in their path. If not directed, they roll across everything that they encounter until they play out and wear down. Ocean waves roll almost endlessly across vast expanses until broken down by things they have impacted along the way. It is much like the principle of light that rolls onward until it reaches its target. In that sense, random waves have random targets and are nonspecific in reaching a certain point. So it is with our conscious thoughts, if random and not focused in a state of heightened awareness, to target a specific point. In most cases, then, our thoughts sort of eke away from us like water leaks, without any direction or specific purpose in mind. They leak all over people, plants, animals, and walls around us, simply making things damp. With little focus and impact, they leave everything in their wake with a feeling of dampness or cold clamminess, infused by the emotional energy that encapsulated them as thoughts formed without much focused intent powered by mental energy.

As a result, most thoughts that are unfocused and roll out aimlessly in waves that spill from us with emotion do not communicate much other than a general impression of the energies that formed the initial thoughts. So our thoughts leave people and other things in their wake with sadness, giddiness, greed, anger, and other emotions that spill out of us without any sort of intelligent focus.

IDLE CONSCIOUSNESS AND WAYWARD THOUGHTS

As I argued in a related book, *Manifesting*, our thoughts are formed out of our consciousness. We will return our focus again to Annie Besant and Charles Leadbeater's work for a deeper analysis of the significance of their studies on thought forms and thought power. These early Theosophical writers examined the actual form of thoughts as they leave a person, and just how these conscious thought forms reach their targets on impact.

Here, we refer again to human consciousness in the context of meditation in heightened awareness. This is consciousness at a focused level that is above the normal functioning of our physical brain and above what many commonly call our mind.

Our personal consciousness with its natural connection to our higher self or spirit can exist outside our body and outside space and time. That enables us to experience out-of-body travel in vivid, lucid dreaming, as previously discussed. It explains our precognition and occasional flashbacks of past lives. It is your very soul essence that you will take with you when you transition beyond the physical plane in mortal death to enter the pure energy world of spirit. We should therefore think about our higher consciousness as insightful awareness that allows us to transcend our physical senses and limited physical sense of space-time.

Besant and Leadbeater analyzed thought forms projected out of our consciousness and saw that they are laced with the colors associated with the energy waves or frequencies we exhibit from our emotional, mental, spiritual, and other energy planes. The various colors of energy have different properties and have a different impact upon arrival. In total, we are a combination of all of the aspects of our many subtle bodies and the energy vortexes that drive them. This is because we are connected to many planes of reality and existence.

The various colors of conscious energy that project from us blur together in swirls that take on colorful hues. That is due to the blending of various energies from different parts of our total being from different energy centers. Gifted aura readers will note how colors leave our outer shells in blended combinations. You will not see all one color distinctly, but in combinations that contribute energy to our thought forms.

These forms leave our body either intentionally or with focus awareness. Let us examine colors of energy that emerge simultaneously from one subtle energy body and two chakras within us. Human desire emanates from the root chakra, while creative intent emanates from the sacral chakra and causal body. Their energies can combine as a swirl of red with perhaps some orange light. The red might come from the base or root chakra, but the orange color of energy comes more from our higher desire in the creative center of our causal body. Or, as previously mentioned, you might see the causal body emitting orange light energy swirled and blended with soft yellow light from the mental plane in a combination of creative and mental energy.

As a reminder, with focused intent you can learn to package the energy that drives your thoughts in creative visualization. Hence, your combined energized consciousness with input from various subtle energy bodies and energy centers can give your thoughts lightning impact with meaningful change. The challenge is to learn to picture what you want to do and how you can best engineer it. Creative visualization at its core is really effectively engineering our imagination and driving it with a picture of what we want to achieve, laced with the power to make it happen. The power behind your thought forms does not simply drive the thoughts to their target but empowers the change to take place upon impact.

You need to project the right energy to give your conscious energy impact as it leaves your body. You need to control your thoughts. This will give you the sort of light energy that you need to effect change. Always remember that each color of light has different properties and corresponds to different planes of existence. It was previously thought by pioneers in thought forms, such as Besant and Leadbeater, that the energy vibrations in our focused thought transference were strongest and tightest as waves closest to the sender.

That leads one to believe that there is a definite though vague range of effect thought transference. It does seem more effective on the whole to be close to the subject you want to receive your thought forms and affect with thought power. If you experiment with sending thought forms, you will probably discover that it is usually easier with the target in the room or when there are numerous senders of the same message. The vibrations are strongest. But we know now that the vibrations continue for some distance. You have probably at some time picked up on someone sending you thought forms. Another mammal, the whale, is known to send messages to others around the world across an entire ocean or even from one ocean to another.

Thoughts not only have form, but they have power. While the colors might swirl with complexity as they are formed out of the mental plane or the emotional plane of the people as senders, the color correspondences in this revealing book are nonetheless worth reviewing:

LIGHT BLUE: High spirituality
SLIGHTLY DARKER BLUE: Devotion as a noble ideal
MEDIUM BLUE: Pure religious feeling
DARK BLUE TINGED WITH GREEN: Religious feeling tinged with fear
DENSE BLUE WITH SWIRLS OF LIGHTER BLUE: Selfish religious feeling
DARK PURPLE: Devotion mixed with affection
LIGHT GREEN: Sympathy
MEDIUM GREEN: Adaptability
MUDDY GREEN: Selfishness
YELLOW: Highest intellect
LIGHT ORANGE: Strong intellect
DARKER ORANGE: Low type of intellect
REDDISH PINK: Pride
SOFT PINK: Love for humanity
MEDIUM PINK: Unselfish affection
DARKER PINK: Pure affection
HOT RED: Avarice

THE RIPPLE THEORY IN COMMUNICATION

Let us overlay our discussion of runaway thoughts with what communication study calls the ripple theory. The Roper ripple theory examines how communication emits outward in all directions in ripples that travel far from the source in all directions but decrease in power like ripples on a pond. Think of dropping a pebble in a relatively still pond and then observing the natural effect of ripples that roll outward. Multiple pebbles dropped into the pond form overlapping concentric circles. Of course, a giant rock dropped in the middle of a still pond could realistically create huge waves in all directions. But to think of our common thoughts with a lack of focus and intent to drive them with power and impact, the kind of wave action we create in the world around us is more like little ripples created by small pebbles dropped into the water.

Let's look again at wave theory from the viewpoint of a person who is standing on the beach, trying to avoid getting wet by timing the waves that splash periodically up to shoe level. Trying to keep from getting soaked by unwanted saltwater, the beachcomber tries to determine the wave pattern by how long it takes the next, similar wave to reach that point on the beach. The beachcomber gets a sense of rhythm, with every wave spaced equally and every wave the same force.

But then something unexpected happens to our tidy beachcomber. Every so often, seemingly out of the blue, a stronger wave pushes forward and messes things up. How can this happen? Isn't there a reliable pattern to wave action?

The answer is yes. However, there can suddenly appear overlapping waves that originated elsewhere, eventually catching up with waves from another source. And then—as frightened sailors with many days at sea will sometimes recount, huge rogue waves come out of nowhere to overcome everything in their way.

If we consider the vastness of the open sea and its many waves coming from various directions, we might grasp an understanding of the overlapping chaos of thought forms that roll across our world. There are many thought forms around us at any given time at any given place. Most of them are weak thought forms with no focus or intent. Most of them are not directed in any direction but just flow outward from the source in all directions like a pebble dropped into the middle of a pond.

So how do we learn to focus and direct our thought forms efficiently to reach a specific target quickly and with impact? And how do we learn to pick one message intended for us specifically from the many runaway messages that are scattered our way and run over us like random waves that overlap each other? It sounds like chaos. It sounds like noise, with competing messages rolling our way.

Well, I have constructed a little exercise that you might practice to single out messages meant specifically for you, and a variation that will help you direct messages through the vast ocean of messages to reach a specific target. It is taken from my own experience.

In 1983, I entered a crowded banquet room where noise made it almost impossible to hear anyone distinctly unless you were pressed against them. Everyone seemed to be talking emphatically in little groups. There was also a clatter of dishes being moved by the waitstaff, and wall speakers carrying music into the room.

Entering this noisy room, I surveyed the crowd and spotted a woman in the far corner with her back to me. Something drew me instantly to her, for reasons I did not immediately understand. I noticed that she was speaking to a woman in the corner. The woman somehow called out to me. I did not seem to know her but had to wonder why she called out to me from across the room with her back to me.

The room suddenly grew quiet inside my head, so that I heard none of the diverse voices. I heard only one person calling out to me—her thoughts inside my head. I sent out the thought that I wanted her to turn around, so I could see why she somehow called out to me. When I drew near, the woman swiveled around abruptly to face me directly. "What is it?" she shouted at me. "What do you want?"

Later she told me that she distinctly heard me call out to her, although I had not uttered a single word and did not even know her. She became an important person in my life and a collaborator in much work I have done since then. How can you single out one message and tune out all others? Maybe the following exercise will help you.

EXERCISE: HEARING ONE VOICE ABOVE A CROWD

NEEDED:

*A room filled with several people who are all speaking at once
*You stand quietly at one end of the room.
*A key person who will attempt to communicate directly with you is standing at the other end of the room.

PROCEDURE:

The key person at the far end of the room from you should close their eyes and attempt to center by tuning out all external and internal distractions. This key person should reach a still point deep within to enter a state of heightened awareness. This person should then begin to focus on you and send a simple message to you telepathically.

You should begin and continue deep, rhythmic breathing. You should close your eyes, centering yourself by tuning out all external and internal distractions to reach a still point deep within you in a state of heightened awareness. You should clear everything inside you to where you see nothing, hear nothing, and think nothing. You are keenly aware and attentive at this point. You are waiting for a single message to come through to you.

Continue this experiment until you feel that you have received a specific message. Confer with the key person at the other end of the room who served as message sender. Tell this person what message you received, to determine how close you came to receiving the message.

VARIATION

Try the same experiment with you in the role as the sender and the key person who initially sent the message as receiver.

NOTE: This isn't easy but can be perfected with practice.

9

A DEAD
MAN'S PHONE

My old boss, Carl Weschcke, wrote a lot about consciousness training and was considered somewhat of an expert in psychic powers. He was also pretty adept on the phone, as I was to learn.

I worked for him for a decade at Llewellyn Worldwide, one of the largest independent publishers in metaphysical literature. Carl owned the publishing house and served as its publisher for many years after acquiring the publishing rights to Welsh astrologer Llewellyn George's annual *Moon Sign Book* and shipping all materials relating to that almanac and Llewellyn George's astrology books to Minnesota from the West Coast on a railroad car back in the 1950s. A few years ago, Carl Weschcke died after an extended illness and left behind many sad friends around the world. I was just one of them. Another was his old secretary Marjorie Toliver.

Marjorie had a special relationship with Carl over the years and a special level of communication with him. Apparently that communication didn't end with Carl's death. To understand how Carl might call Marjorie after his death, you need to know a little bit more about the ties that bound them together so tightly throughout the years. Marjorie was the secretary for Carl's father before she was Carl's secretary. When Carl started Llewellyn Worldwide, Marjorie found him the perfect building to house both his publishing operation and his family. The three-and-a-half-story mansion in historic Saint Paul, Minnesota, had been a cultural center and was available by auction. Marjorie figured out the right bid for Carl to get the historic building at a very good price. She then served the new publishing company as Carl's secretarial assistant, a position she had held earlier in his father's business. They found that they had many things in common and served on some of the same civil rights, cultural, and political organizations. When Carl married and had a child, Marjorie took on a role that brought her even closer to Carl and the family. She cared for the child while his father and mother worked at the growing publishing company. She took the young son on walks and play trips around town and cared for him for several years. Marjorie had no other close family, so she became like a part of Carl's family. This relationship continued for several decades until both Marjorie and Carl entered their senior years.

Carl's knees gave out in his declining years, so he stopped going into the office every day. He would go into the office a few days each week to meet with staff and conduct business, depending more and more on his wife and son. That is sort of when I knew Carl, working for him and his wife in those transitional years.

Carl was a huge presence in presiding over our many staff meetings on acquisitions, vision, marketing, reprints, cover design, budgeting, and the myriad of other functions that are part of book publishing. He seemed to love human interaction and genuinely enjoy meeting with authors and others in the many stages of publishing. He loved to talk and loved the human exchange of dialogue and open discussion. With two periodicals and a hundred books to publish every year, he had a lot of human interaction. And the longer the discussions, the more he seemed to enjoy them. Carl loved to talk to people, especially the people he knew and shared his work.

Eventually, Carl began staying home every day and working apart from the office. He turned his attention to writing his own books, after decades of publishing the books of other people and distributing them around the world. And his books on consciousness development and developing psychic powers held a world of useful information after his years in publishing and personal study. The books have been well received and popular.

Carl's lifeline then became his telephone. He would call me to invite me to lunch at his home and make specific suggestions about what kind of pizza and what kind of sandwiches I should bring. He was always a great communicator, even before his writing days, and could get people to do almost anything when he got them on the phone. In his basement study and library, Carl could reach out to a broad world of people he knew and cared about. He was just a phone call away.

Carl told me once when I worked for him in Saint Paul about his old friend and secretary, Marjorie, the woman he had trusted to care for his son in his early years at home. Carl and his wife tried to figure the point at which Marjorie decided she no longer needed a regular job at the company and would work on her own. Marjorie had acquired rental property. She eventually acquired two apartment buildings, both nearby. She lived in one of the buildings. When she had enough renters, she decided to stay home and manage her properties. But she maintained contact with Carl, her old friend. So, Carl always seemed to know where Marjorie was with Festival of Nations, NAACP, and other programs that competed for her time.

Despite knowing about Marjorie from talking with Carl, I never met her until shortly before Carl's death. Carl hooked us up and initiated our meeting. Carl called me from his new home in Woodbury to tell me that his old friend Marjorie needed help. He thought of me. I was flattered. People were generally flattered when Carl thought of them and spoke with them.

He pointed out that since retiring from Llewellyn, I was now engaged as a landlord, much like Marjorie. So, he thought that I could help. Marjorie struggled in her old age with a series of setbacks and challenges. One of her two small apartment buildings, Carl told me, had roof damage from heavy snow that led to extensive water leaks to the apartments below. As a result, Marjorie had vacant rental units. She herself had to move to the other building. She was using some of the vacant apartments to store office supplies and papers. As a result, she had extensive repair expenses on top of lost revenue. Her records were all piled up in a couple of empty rooms, and she was not able to keep up with the business on a lot of levels. She needed someone to organize her bills, get remodeling on track, and sign up new renters once the rooms could be readied for occupancy. It was a lot of work for an elderly woman who had found it easy enough to manage before the roof literally caved in on her. On top of that, Carl's old friend was a bit of a hoarder and had clothes dating back to her high school years and stacks of old newspapers and magazines piled everywhere in the basement.

Carl told me to meet with Marjorie and give her some help with her two apartment buildings. Because it was Carl, who was impossible to ignore and always compelling when he spoke, I said yes. I had no right to say yes. I was already spread too thin. But nobody liked to disappoint Carl. He was that convincing and that charming. Getting Marjorie to agree to meet with someone to poke around her business after years of working alone was not easy. But she was as charming as Carl in her own way, so I persisted until we set a time to meet.

We met outside one of her apartment buildings. We toured every room and hallway in both buildings and then surveyed them from the outside, examining where they needed exterior work and improved parking. They were beautiful, older apartment buildings but were largely vacant from the recent problems Marjorie had suffered. She was sweet and impressive but also a bit guarded, as any self-made entrepreneur who had never needed much outside help is likely to appear after several years. I made some general observations about what directions I would take, but then admitted that my time was limited now and I was not certain that I could spend the time to help her organize things. When I got home, I thought of my good friend and renter Ricky Foos, who had some accounting experience and had experience as a property owner. He was an older fellow like me and retired, so that he had a little free time available. Fortunately, Ricky displayed interest in a part-time, low-paying job helping Marjorie.

The next problem was convincing Marjorie to meet with Ricky, whom she had never met. So, I called Carl and impressed on him that Marjorie needed to be convinced. As I mentioned earlier, Carl was very convincing on the phone. So, he called Marjorie back and convinced her to meet about turning her business over to a total stranger who was recommended by a friend of a friend. Marjorie called me to set up a time for Ricky to visit her. Ricky made the trip alone, a total stranger knocking on her door. Fortunately, they formed a working relationship, thanks to Carl's persuasiveness. In short order, Ricky was sorting things out with her at Marjorie's two buildings five days a week. It was not easy, and some things they encountered in sorting things out were downright confusing.

One thing that confused both of them was the strange thing that appeared out of thin air shortly after Carl died. Marjorie was heartbroken, like many people, over Carl's passing and had attended his memorial service. She missed her old friend and thought of him daily. She missed his advice and his concern. She missed his voice on the phone. One day she entered her apartment with Ricky and found a strange telephone sitting on her kitchen table. She noticed it immediately and exclaimed to Ricky that she had no idea where the phone came from or why it was there. She did not recognize it. So, she examined it closely. It was an older-style black telephone, a desk phone. There was a note on the side. It was one of those address labels that listed your name and street address. The label clearly listed the name Carl Weschcke and his home address. At the bottom of the address label, Carl had written his phone number in black ink. It was clearly written by Carl's own hand, since he had distinctive handwriting.

Marjorie put the phone away. She did not attempt to use it. She did not connect it. The idea of speaking to her old friend who had since passed on made her nervous. I asked Marjorie why she did not try speaking on the phone. She just shook her head. In trying to determine how that phone had appeared out of nowhere to land on a table inside her apartment, however, she never reached an explanation. It seemed possible that Carl had reached out from the spirit realm and placed the phone for her. No other explanation came to mind. Nobody ever provided clues or details. Nobody admitted giving her the phone or placing it there. It remains a mystery to this day.

From what I have learned about spirit communication in doing research for this book, I believe that I would have tried using the phone. It might have provided startling results, even if it were not connected to a phone line. It might have a recorded message. Or it might have been a straight line of communication to Marjorie's old friend.

I wanted to see the phone myself. Ricky took a photo of it and sent it to me. Intrigued, I went over to Marjorie's place to see it myself. Something told me that the phone would not work for me, Ricky, or anyone other than Marjorie. The phone seemed to be a link between Carl and Marjorie only. You have to respect that. And you have to respect Marjorie's personal decision not to pick up the receiver.

Since Marjorie's discovery of the phone and speaking with her and Ricky about it, I have spoken to Carl's wife about it. She told me that she knows nothing about it. In fact, she was surprised to hear about the phone's appearance. She had no clues or observations about the phone, only that it was a startling mystery to all. She did not recall any phone at home or in Carl's possessions that had disappeared. She could not imagine any practical, physical explanation for its appearance in Marjorie's apartment. To my knowledge, Carl did not send any personal effects to Marjorie (with the possible exception of one black desk phone). He did not make arrangements for any of his personal items or other articles for Marjorie. All that Marjorie seemed to receive after his passing was a mysterious black telephone with his name on it.

There is a long history of anecdotal information about the dead reaching out by telephone to those they loved. Sometimes the phone was not even a working phone. The phone that mysteriously appeared on Marjorie's desk one day was not connected. It had no established phone service or network connection. There was no attached answering machine. It simply appeared in her private quarters with an old friend's name on it. And to this day, nobody seems to know how it got there or why it was placed there. Knowing both Carl and Marge as I do, however, I have to believe that Carl wanted one last word with his old friend.

Now I must bring this little story to a personal level for you. Have you ever had a phone call where you could not really distinguish what was said to you? Have you ever received a call that had a lot of bizarre static or a distant voice you could not easily hear? Maybe the phone rang, and nobody seemed to be there. Now I must ask you whether these little mysteries were ever resolved for you. Did you subsequently hear that someone you know and speak with tried to call you but could not get a clear line? Or do you still just shake your head and call that a little mystery? Maybe mysteries like that happen more than we think, because we have no frame of reference in our physical world to help us resolve the matter and put them to rest. So, we just ignore them as anomalies. But have you ever wondered whether a loved one or old friend who has died wanted one last word with you? Sometimes I think it is entirely possible that I could dial a phone number of someone I once knew and reach them, even though that number might be long since disconnected. It is really just a matter of making yourself receptive and ready to receive a call, should someone from beyond really want to contact you. Sometimes I go through motions in my mind to call my mother at our old phone number. That house that has long been torn down to make way for industry. In fact, the entire phone line there has been removed, as all houses in that area gave way to new industry.

Other times, I think about calling up to Alaska, where I once operated a busy community newspaper. I even think about dialing my first home to see if my bride is still there. I know we're still listed in some old phone books there. I know that such connections could be possible. The spirit realm does not follow our flow of time but operates outside time and space, as we experience it in our physical realm. I suggest that you try it yourself. Try it every now and then just to see what might happen. It costs you nothing. At the very least, it's a nice way to remember someone near and dear to you. You might even give them a chance to reach out to you, if that is what they want.

Try this little exercise:

EXERCISE: JUST PICK UP THE PHONE

NEEDED:

*A telephone. (To make this easier and improve your chances of success, I suggest that you have a working phone that is currently hooked to a network. It can be a desk phone, a wall phone, or even a cell phone. It is probably best if you use this phone regularly and it's imprinted with you by repeated use. But you could also try this experiment with a phone that is not a working phone or one that is connected to a network.)

*You might want to be sitting down when you do this exercise. So, I would suggest the ideal setting would be a straight-back chair that you occupy with a table in front of you.

*Wear loose-fitting clothing, with shoes and jewelry removed, to make it more comfortable for you to enter a meditative state and let energy flow freely through your body.

PROCEDURE:

Sit erect in the chair with your feet firmly grounded. (If you are not using a chair, then the best meditative approach would be for you to recline on your back faceup, with your legs and arms extended at 45-degree angles. This is called the classic dead-man pose in yoga.) Fix your attention on the phone near you and think about somebody calling you. Put yourself in a state of heightened consciousness by tuning out all internal and external distractions and reaching a still point deep within you. Begin and continue deep, rhythmic breathing.

Close your eyes and picture someone you know and miss. See that person clearly on a screen before your mind's eye. Wait to see if the phone rings. If it does not ring, wait awhile and pick up the receiver.

Speak into the phone in your normal voice. Say, "Hello. I am here. Can you hear me?"

NOTES: I am not suggesting that you attempt to contact the dead or anyone from the spirit realm. Perhaps a live person will pick up on your receptivity and call you. You are simply making yourself open and receptive to receiving a call from beyond. These are rare, and you might not receive one. But I think it's entirely possible that you might sometime.

10

THREE MYSTERIOUS PHONE CALLS IN WHEATON

Several years ago, I received a series of mysterious phone calls that changed my life forever. I was working at the national headquarters of the international Theosophical Society in Wheaton, Illinois, at the time. In fact, I had just started working there before the first call rang through to me. The calls were unusual in that I was new there and didn't know the caller, who seemed nonetheless to know me. I was just working quietly in my corner office upstairs in the Theosophical Publishing House building, surrounded by hot houseplants. My corner room, with windows all around it, faced south and drew intense sunlight in the afternoon. Consequently, I started placing potted plants that love the sun on the windowsills. With so many aloe veras and other plants growing to immense size as they basked in the sun, that room began to feel like a jungle enclosure more than the corner office of a book publisher. I stayed busy up there, and the phone seldom rang. Then one day all of that changed. The phone rang in the middle of the afternoon, and I heard what sounded like the voice of an elderly man from India. The accent was quite thick, but I could easily understand him. The connection was extremely clear on the landline phone.

"Good day, sir!" he said. "I am calling you today to invite you on my lightning tour of India!"

He told me that he led a tour of India in the fall every year, usually in September. He said that was the best time, although he had done it also in late August. I asked him who he was. He ignored that question and continued to explain that he was the person who organized the lightning tours of India. So, I asked him how he got my name and why he had called me specifically. He simply answered that it was something I needed and that it would change my life. I began to think that he had intended to call my predecessor there at the publishing house, Clarence "Pete" Pederson, who had recently retired after many years as publications director of the American section of the society. So, I asked my caller if he was calling for Pete. He reaffirmed that he was calling for me, and that his offer was something that I needed to hear. He continued to sell the benefits of touring India with him in the fall and encouraged me to make the time to join him.

I tried to explain to the persistent old man that I was new in my job and could not take time off for a vacation. He countered that it was not exactly a vacation, but a spiritual adventure. So I told him how busy I was in my new job. I had helped launch many new projects at our national headquarters that had all of us quite busy. We had started a self-syndicated radio program that went out to thirty-seven stations nationwide, and a self-syndicated television program based on author interviews that went out to thirteen TV stations across the country. In addition, we had launched a new magazine, *The Quest*, and also organized some high-profile weekend lectures in Chicago. I found myself walking in pajamas to the office from my bedroom in another part of the building on many nights just to try to keep up. So, the idea of taking a two-day tour of India in the fall didn't seem practical just then. After explaining all of that to my elderly caller as diplomatically as I could without sounding ungrateful, he simply responded with upbeat enthusiasm that he would call me again after I had a chance to give the offer due consideration. He repeated that it would be a life-altering experience that I could not miss.

Puzzled by this strange call, I tried to make some sense of it afterward. I considered that it was logical for someone from India to call our national headquarters, since the international headquarters of the Theosophical Society is located in southern India. Many of our leading teachers are elderly Indian mystics, since the society is steeped in Eastern spiritual science. I went to the other building to quiz our information officer, who took incoming calls and routed them. Maybe she could shed some light on the identity of my caller. But she told me that she had not routed any such call to me, and that the Indian gentleman had apparently dialed my extension directly. She said that she would certainly remember such a caller had she routed the call. So I considered that the phone call might have been a hoax as some practical joke played on me by somebody on staff. I walked throughout our two buildings relating the story to various people, in hopes they might confess or give it away with blinking eyes or funny grins. I discussed the call with people on staff whose voices seemed somewhere in the range of my caller or close enough that they might have been able to fake the voice of an elderly man with a thick Indian accent. Everyone seemed baffled by such a strange story, however. Nobody seemed to give any clue whatsoever that they knew anything about the call.

So, I just sort of forgot about this little mystery, since I had no other way to deal with it. I put it out of my mind and did not think about the old Indian mystic again until his next call. A week or so later, he rang me again. It was late afternoon and I was working in the office when the desk phone rang. I recognized the voice of the elderly Indian gentleman immediately and again asked his name and how he had singled me out. He disregarded these questions as though he did not hear them. Instead, he told me again about the wonders of joining him on his annual lightning tour of India in the fall and why I should agree to participate. Again, I explained that I was new there and had no vacation time and plenty of work to keep me busy in the months ahead. But I thanked him for the offer. I asked him for details of the trip and how he selected his group each year, but he seemed to disregard those questions as well. Again, he told me that it was a great opportunity that would be life changing for me and that I should think some more about it.

He did not say goodbye. He simply stopped talking. Looking back, it did not seem that the phone line clicked, as though he had disconnected. The voice simply stopped, and I was left with silence. So, I hung up and figured that I would never hear from him again after telling him no twice. But I was wrong, because he did give me a third chance. A week or so later, he called again and made the very same offer. He offered no additional information or explanation. But when I told him no again, he added something. He told me that it was unfortunate if I could not accompany him on a lightning tour of India, but he could still give me some insight that would also change my life forever. He told me that I should learn to meditate in the early-morning light next to running water. I told him that I had learned to meditate, but he said that meditating next to running water in the first light of day was the best way to meditate. He did not explain how it would be better, but he did give me the steps to meditate in this way. I told him that we had a pond out back on the grounds where I could meditate. He did not acknowledge this statement but simply outlined the approach. He said that I should lay a blanket or something on the ground and sit there quietly to begin meditating. I should become one with the morning light. I should practice that daily until I learned to live in the light and move in the light.

MOVING IN THE LIGHT

I began to practice the special meditation technique prescribed for me by the Indian sage. Since he was apparently Indian, old, and familiar with the Theosophical Society, I guessed that he must be Hindu and schooled in yoga. At that time, I had never heard of this approach to yoga or meditation. But it seemed easy enough to try.

I spread a bicentennial blanket given to me as a gift on the grass beside the pond in the back of our campus. It stood under huge trees and contained many fish that looked rather lethargic in the summer heat. There was little running water in the pond at that time, but I figured that it was a handy place to get started. As I understood the advice from my mystery caller, this sort of meditation would work best beside a stream, a waterfall, or perhaps the beach with the waves rushing toward me. But the location that was handy for me was comfortable and tranquil. As a meditation place, it was ideal for its solitude in the early morning and certainly caught the morning light beside the pond.

I began to notice a difference in my meditations almost immediately. I could feel the light not only on my physical body, but deep within me. Meditating in the morning light, I felt the warmth and power of the energy running through me throughout my entire being on all levels. I felt one with the light. I could sense that there was something special about the new light of day too. Because the old Indian's advice on meditating in the light was impressive, I wanted to learn if anyone else was practicing meditation in this manner. So, one Saturday morning I went into our Quest Bookshop on the first floor of our publication building and talked to our bookstore manager, Shirley Spears. I asked Shirley where the serious books by Hindu masters were located in the shop. There were many books on yoga and meditation, but I wanted to see what the real Indian masters thought about meditating in the morning light next to running water. Shirley simply pointed to one corner of the shop, where the good stuff was on display.

When I reached the shop's corner where these specific books were gathered, I noticed one book that was displayed face-out on a book stand. It stood out from all of the other books there. So, I picked it up and saw a picture of an old man, a yogi master. Curious about this man and his book, I flipped the book over to read the back-cover copy. It spoke about a man who taught a special technique for meditating in the early-morning light next to running water. Toward the bottom, it stated that he was also famous for his annual lightning tours of India in the fall. At the very bottom, it listed the old man's date of birth and also his date of death. Yes, the man had died a couple of years ago. If this was the man who had called me, he had called me from beyond the grave.

It's unusual, I know, for ghostly phone calls or any form of spirit communication to be as elaborate and verbal as my phone calls. My mystery man spoke clearly in complete sentences. I heard his voice very clearly, probably more clearly than typical transcontinental phone calls on landlines back then. He seemed to interact with me in his conversation to some degree. If his calls were truly beyond the grave, I felt particularly privileged that he sought me out. I feel even better about the fact that he gave me good meditation advice that has broad significance in moving in the light. My special interest in time and space benefited from this knowledge and practice.

PUTTING A SPIRIT'S ADVICE TO GOOD USE

The advice on living and moving in the light proved beneficial not only to me, but also to someone special in my life. I was able to apply his meditation technique when I met a woman who was dying of cancer.

I met Deb Bennett shortly after leaving the Theosophical Society's publishing program in Wheaton. I moved to Saint Paul, Minnesota, to work for Carl and Sandra Weschcke at Llewellyn Publications and acquired a three-story classic Victorian house in Saint Paul. I moved into the hundred-year-old house as a roommate shortly after coming to the city. I bought the building a few months later, when the owner decided to move west to Texas.

I ended up with an extra room when the previous owner left me and the other roommates behind. So, I posted an ad in the local newspaper and got a call from Deb (an earlier book called *Moving in the Light: The Deb Bennett Story* discusses my experiences with Deb in depth). She showed up for a rental interview with a couple of cats and a frightening history of cancer. She had gone through lengthy treatment, lost all of her hair, and was pretty much given up for dead by her family. But then she went into some kind of miraculous remission and was declared cancer free. She was even on the radio to discuss her amazing return from cancer.

When she first came to my house, Deb was only thirty-two years old and ready to begin her life again. She was eating and living a healthful lifestyle and said that she looked forward to the rest of her life, now that she was healthy again. It had been a long journey, and Deb said that she had been sick and in recovery for so long that she had never really gone anywhere except for a brief trip to Texas. She loved the television show *Star Trek*, where space travelers could transport their bodies from one location to another. "Beam me up, Scottie!" was one of Deb's favorite lines from the show. She would sit in her wicker rocker in our living room watching the show, while her cat Wizard pulled cat toys out of the wicker basket that she kept there for cat essentials. Deb walked in on me once when I was typing on my old Brother word processor, busy on a book that I wanted to write. I told her that I wanted to call it *Moving in the Light* and discuss an amazing meditation technique I had learned from a mysterious man who used to call me. As it turned out, that book, when finally completed, was more about Deb than anything else. There was something in what the mysterious Indian sage told me on the phone that would play a major part in Deb's story.

You see, Deb's brain tumor had returned. We did not catch it immediately, and even her scheduled lab checkups didn't seem to catch it. But a few months after Deb and her cats moved into my Victorian home, she started stumbling on the stairs. Other times, she appeared to be in a daze. When she started missing time at work, her coworkers from Dayton Hudson in Roseville showed up at our house for an intervention to encourage Deb to return to the hospital for tests. She was in denial, stating emphatically that she had beaten cancer and was clear of it. It was simply a cold, she insisted, but she exhibited no typical symptoms associated with a cold. So, we finally convinced her to let friends from work drive her to Fairview South in Minneapolis.

There we learned that the cancer had returned and was spreading fast. Brain surgeons operated but could not get it all. Consequently, Deb went to Saint John's Hospital in Saint Paul for radiation and chemotherapy. She lost her hair again. It seemed hopeless. We considered hospice care and realized that we could not do it ourselves, since we all worked. So, we asked the Sister Kenny staff who did rehab work in Minneapolis to keep her temporarily until a hospital bed become available somewhere.

At last, sisters of mercy in Saint Paul found Deb a bed at their terminal care center. Somebody had to die there to free up Deb's bed. She was only thirty-two years old and had expected after her earlier miraculous recovery from cancer to be starting a whole new life.

HOW THE PIECES FIT

Her friends, family, and I began visiting Deb at the hospice. So did her cat Wizard, whom she credited earlier with helping her heal when she first had cancer. As before, Wizard would sit on her lap and purr. His body seemed to heat up while she tried to pet him. In time, however, Deb could not even sit up, work her hands, or speak. I would try to take her on walks in a wheelchair when she first got there, set up videos for her to watch, or feed her pizza. But then she became weaker and totally bedridden. It was then that I thought how to apply what the old Indian mystic had told me about moving in the light and living in the light. It occurred to me that the light could take a person beyond normal time and space. I reasoned that becoming one with the light would allow you to travel with the speed of light to other places.

I wondered what other kind of places Deb might want to visit if she had a transporter device like the one on *Star Trek*. Maybe she would like to move beyond the confines of her bed and the restrictions of her physical body. If she could travel like that, riding on the light,

I reasoned, she might transcend mundane space-time. Maybe she could visit other realms of reality.

The pieces begin to form inside my mind. The old Indian mystic knew all about the subtle energy bodies that surround our physical body. He knew that our life force and consciousness exist on all of these levels of our total being, although few people outside of Hindu masters ever experienced them with any kind of focused awareness. So we applied the old Indian master's advice on moving and living in the light to Deb and adapted meditation exercises for her to practice leaving her physical body and traveling in the light. I asked Deb if she remembered my story about moving in the light, and then asked if she wanted to try some meditation exercises to experience that for herself. I told her it might be a lot like stepping into the transporters on *Star Trek* and going somewhere new.

The idea of walking outside that hospice without using her legs and experiencing a fuller life beyond her deathbed appealed to her. So together we tried some meditation exercises in the light. We found just enough natural sunlight crossing her bed from a window at certain times of the day. The hospital had a water fountain. We had everything we needed to move and live in the light. Deb was certainly focused. Anyplace would be better than a deathbed in a hospice, no matter how attentive were the nuns who were her medical attendants.

We entered the light together and moved together in the light. The experience was exhilarating. Deb enjoyed our travels into the light and became comfortable doing these exercises. Soon I sensed that she could do them on her own. When I asked her whether she felt that she could move in the light on her own, she squeezed my hand and said the only word she had uttered in several weeks. "Yes!" she said. I told Sister Luke, head nurse there, that Deb was ready. I knew that Deb would be all right, because she could walk out of that hospice now anytime she wanted. And it was almost unlimited where the light could take her.

Deb died the next morning. I sensed the moment when she died, and stood up with a jolt. I looked around and saw a faint image of Deb playing with Wizard in the living room. She dangled a pink ribbon over his head and then dropped it into her wicker basket. Later, I found a pink ribbon exactly where I had seen her drop it. I had never seen her pink ribbon before. Later, I discovered a whole box of pink ribbons that she was apparently fashioning into Christmas gifts. I heard her stereo coming from her room later that day. When I went inside to investigate, the music stopped. Then I remembered that everything had been removed from her bedroom weeks before by her parents. There was no stereo.

Yes, Deb will be fine now. She learned to move freely in the light and live in the light. I sometimes wonder whether that old Indian sage who called me years before envisioned a day when I could use his meditation training to help my friend Deb. After all, there is no sense of normal time or space in the spirit realm. A person calling me from the spirit realm could probably see into the future.

11

BROTHER'S FRANTIC CALLS TO FAMILY AFTER DEATH

I f you ask enough people about dead relatives who contact them shortly after passing, you begin to hear a consistent story from many of them. This is all anecdotal data, of course, and would be hard to verify any other way than simply interviewing all of the people who claim to have been visited in this fashion. It does appear, nonetheless, that our recently departed friends and relatives often want to contact us shortly after passing from this physical plane to a spiritual realm, and many apparently find ways to do so.

Take the example of my close friends on the West Coast and the strange calls they received after a family member had recently died. The calls went to the dead man's sister and were subsequently heard by five family members who seemed to agree about the source of the mysterious calls. The dead man's sister called me shortly after receiving the calls and provided shocking details. I have subsequently interviewed her family members who heard the phone messages. Their accounts have not changed over time; the memories of the calls appear seared into their minds.

While I am convinced by the authenticity of these apparent spirit communications, given the amount of collaboration and details, I am masking the identity of the people who heard the calls. I was asked not to identify them, since they do not want to personally expose themselves to public attention. Consequently, I will refer to the sister of the dead man here as "Tess." The calls came on a home landline. It is fair to say that their relationship for many years had been rocky, for reasons best known to them. I had known the man who died for his whole life and worked with him a while too.

The dead brother had been injured years earlier while he was on active duty in the US Army. He was stationed in Vietnam, but the injury occurred when he returned stateside and was loading a truck. The tail flap of the big truck apparently fell onto his head, when he was bent over to grab items on the ground behind it. He was hospitalized as a result, but the extent of his head injuries was not immediately known. When he was released from the Army, the young man sort of drifted, often unable to hold a full-time job for long because of his injuries. The head injury caused spinal damage and tremendous nerve pain. In fact, he complained that he would be fine one minute and then become numb on one side of his body the next. The headaches must have been staggering. Oh, he would try to work in whatever way he could, but he often found it to be too much to handle after a few days on the job. We all probably wondered whether he would live much longer.

He received disability insurance from the Veterans Administration, but then that level of coverage was cut when government administrations changed, and every check was held up to serious scrutiny. In truth, this man did compile a sort of work history after his injury during Army service, but he was never strong enough to keep any of these jobs very long. I'm afraid that simply trying to work hurt his disability coverage in the end, since he was considered able to get jobs.

This injured veteran was probably not a great communicator, looking back at his problems getting along with his sister and me. He began to move around the country from state to state. He took what little money he could gather to buy a junked ice cream truck in hopes of working it. That didn't pan out. He tried buying old buildings for rental property but had trouble collecting rent and maintaining the properties with the type of renters these inexpensive dwellings would attract. Along the way, people who had known him for years didn't get phone calls, letters, or even cards. He communicated through his mother when he wanted to have someone speak with him. He would have her wrangle somebody onto the phone and then relay his message through her. Things seemed to take a dark turn after his injury.

He was not always like that, going back to his boyhood days. He would follow a group of older kids in the neighborhood to go fishing across town. He was an adventurous tot, even when he was only five or six years old. He could take care of himself back then. I recall that he was once professionally photographed fishing at bayside docks on his knees. The large photo appeared in a full-page ad for fishing line in *Outdoor Life* magazine. As a sophomore, he made the high school football team as a receiver at his suburban high school. And then a couple of years later, he was in the Army, headed for Vietnam. A lot of people returned from Vietnam with lingering problems of one sort or another. When his veterans disability pension was reduced, he tried working at a fish-and-chips restaurant. He was found on the floor one night after collapsing while attempting to mop the floor all alone after-hours.

He kept pushing, however, trying to stay active. He took ski lessons, and we went skiing together. He was the better skier, absolutely fearless and daring. He moved to Alaska, where he worked awhile as a photographer, following the local Gold Medal basketball team around the state. He loved boating up there. I remember seeing a photo of him digging clams enthusiastically, a front-page photo in a small-town Alaskan newspaper.

Communication between this Army veteran and his sister seemed to really sour when their mother developed Alzheimer symptoms and gave power of attorney over to her daughter. Her brother removed their mother from nursing-home care and wrested power of attorney from his sister. That made him his mother's caretaker. He had trouble caring for himself but still wanted to care for his mother. He took his mother miles away from his sister to live with him in another state. They lived in the Midwest in one of the brother's rundown rental properties. Eventually, the mother had to be placed in a nursing home that handled many Alzheimer patients there. The brother visited her at the nursing home, but she did not really recognize people well at that point. And there she died. Then he was all alone. And one morning, his girlfriend came to call on him and found him lying dead on the floor in his house.

But his story did not end there. Neither did the fight between the brother and sister. She was to hear from him again, apparently, and so were others in the family. I was notified when he died, since I knew people there pretty well. A local mortuary where he was taken called to ask me what should be done with him. With no local family and both his parents deceased, officials in this small town had tried to handle details of his demise as best they could. They accessed his local bank account to accommodate his final expenses. So, I suggested that they allow a few days for local friends there to organize whatever memorial service they might want. I remember working with local officials there to keep his body more or less on ice for several days to allow for viewing and services. I have no way of knowing how many people actually visited him or remembered him in his final days there.

A couple of days after he died, however, his sister back on the West Coast began receiving alarming phone calls that were left as recorded phone messages. The person at the other end of her calls didn't identify himself but only screamed and swore at her in muffled recordings. She thought she recognized the words and the voice. She called me to say that it sounded like her brother was calling her from beyond the grave and yelling at her on the telephone. She said that the voice messages were muffled like white noise.

"He said 'mom' over and over again and also 'bitch,'" the woman told me. The last call, he screamed "Fire!" and "Burning!" She added that that was the day she understood her dead brother had been put into the ground at the cemetery. She said that she never received another similar message after that. She said that she turned the phone messages over to her husband, two daughters, and son-in-law so they could listen to the strange calls.

"They were convinced it was his voice," she said of her dead brother.

She said that the messages were saved as voice messages but then strangely disappeared without a trace. "I thought the messages would save," she said, "but after a while they disappeared."

Fortunately, she said, her husband took notes while the messages were still saved in her phone bank. Her journalist husband tells a similar story, but with a slightly personal twist.

"Throughout my life," he told me, "I have been a believer in the paranormal but have generally leaned more toward skepticism and logic. I can count on one hand the number of times I've come across unexplained phenomena, but they didn't leave a lasting impression on me. This is the only paranormal encounter I've had involving a phone call that surfaced without warning but seemed timely to events that just happened."

He told me that the voice sounded like someone who was in agonizing pain and trying to be heard over a severe rain and windstorm. He said that the voice on the recorded phone message said "mom" a few times and the word "fire." He said that the messages at times included what sounded like screams. At other times, the phone messages included "incomplete syllables or phrases that were unintelligible." He agreed with his wife that there was a lot of white noise, "like when TVs went off the air at night in the old days. It was constant from start to finish," he said of the noise, "and only occasionally could the voice be heard just slightly more than the static."

The journalist husband confirmed that the messages were received on the couple's cordless phone, which had voicemail as an add-on service. "It wasn't the kind with a minicassette," he said, "so the calls weren't something we thought we necessarily had to save. Basically, you could go in and check your voicemails, and we had no reason to think that the phone company would delete them at a later date. The two message calls I remember were just there for a couple of weeks, then they weren't." He insists that neither he nor his wife deleted them. He said that he took notes at the time of the calls, however, and put them into a Word file.

Before the calls were deleted, he and his wife had other family members listen to them. He said that they all listened to them together a couple of times. "We didn't want them to think we were imagining it or hearing things," he said. "I remember they were as chilled as we were."

If the calls to Tess were indeed from her deceased brother, it would seem strange that her brother in the Midwest even knew her phone number. They had not spoken in some time. When I heard about the woman's mysterious phone calls, I was naturally alarmed. It suggested that the woman's dead brother was not at peace, but tormented. It also suggested that he wanted to attack people he knew in his time of pain and anguish. How long could that go on? How could we put an end to such calls?

As soon as I heard about the first phone call from the man's sister, I called the mortuary in the town where the man had died. I asked the mortician how soon her brother could be cremated, and his ashes buried. I was told that the body would need to be sent out of state, where he could receive a military burial in a Veterans Administration cemetery.

His body was sent within a day, and when the brother's remains were cremated, the phone calls stopped. There have been no other calls of that sort to this day, several years later. There was just one last phone call to the sister a couple days after the body was sent out of state for cremation. She told me that she received a similar call where the caller didn't identify himself but just started yelling. It sounded like the same voice. It sounded like her dead brother.

This time, the message was a little different. Instead of berating his sister with derisive slurs and calling her many offensive names, the voice yelled out that he was burning. He screamed as though in pain and complained about the fire. I found this report from Tess to be most interesting. You see, I had not told her that I had arranged for her brother to be transported for cremation. When I heard that the sister received this final strange phone call, it all made sense. That final strange call to the dead man's sister corresponded perfectly to the time of his cremation. We cannot pinpoint the time precisely but can figure that it was when the body was being cremated or just before or after cremation. After that, no more such calls reached the man's sister.

Sadly, there were no phone calls with parting words of love or sorrow to anyone from the dead man. Only angry calls to his sister, whom he seemed to detest. I cannot recite some of the foul language the dead man seemed to throw at his sister—only that it includes some very personal comments that she would uniquely remember and recognize. They were vulgar obscenities that cannot be printed here. Sometimes I wonder why the dead man called only his sister and not me or anyone else. Surely, many people might have disappointed him many times along the way. After his Army accident and years of crippling pain, few people had significantly helped him with his many unfulfilled dreams and projects or encouraged him with his investment projects, none of which seemed to work out well.

In fact, toward the end of his life, local people criticized the level of care he gave to his ailing mother. Social Services investigated his home care of her and tried to take his mother out of his control. Police got involved. There were other investigations into sanitation and care of animals at his properties there. Finally, an officer of the court visited the house shared by him and his mother and said that declining health dictated a change of direction. His mother was taken from him and put into a nursing home for professional care. And that is where she died, just shortly before her son died alone in his home in the same town.

Now, these mysterious calls to the dead man's sister at her house came over the phone directly and, in her absence, went into recorded voicemail. All of these calls were recorded on her home landline and remained for some time as recorded voicemail. The recorders were played for both of Tess's daughters, her son-in-law, and her husband. Every one of these family members who heard them, according to Tess and her husband, thought the voice on the recorded messages sounded like Tess's deceased brother.

Tess's husband, who knew police in the area, asked a commander on the local police force whether the lost phone messages could somehow be retrieved. Curiously, however, no clue has surfaced to explain what happened to the recording. Nobody I asked said they had deleted it. It simply vanished after a few days without a trace.

Now this is again anecdotal evidence supplied by witnesses. In this case, I would submit that the dead man's sister and members of her family should be able to identify the dead relative's voice after knowing him for many years. And what the caller said to his sister seemed very personal and targeted for her ears only. Typically, it seems that ghost callers do not identify themselves. Maybe they no longer feel that they have that same personal identity as a spirit and are no longer a living person. Typically, ghost callers do not have a dialogue exchange but tend to deliver messages without leaving the room for replies or discussion. They seem to be on an urgent mission to deliver a message. That seems to be true of the sister's mysterious messages from beyond as well.

Nobody at the receiving end could get in a word or make a comment that was recognized by the caller. Now, the part of the sister's ghost calls that I find especially interesting is how her brother was nowhere near a telephone and did not have his sister's phone number. Again, I would suggest that spirits do not really need to have telephones to make phone calls. All they seem to require for you to get their message is for you to have a phone.

And they probably resort to calling on a phone only because that's the way people expect to be contacted from a distance. They could probably just as easily put the message in your head for you alone to hear.

Tess was not on any sort of speaking terms with her brother, however. They had nothing good to say to each other and chose to keep a distance. That's why the calls from someone who sounded like her deceased brother seemed so startling to her. Especially after he had died. We need to think of the emotional and mental energy that drives our conscious thought forms. Our emotional and mental planes of existence, these subtle energy bodies that surround our dense, physical body, can operate on their own. They do not need a brain to send them an impulse. The impulse comes from emotional and mental energy that exists outside the physical body. Consciousness exists on all planes of existence and all subtle body levels, driven by impulse from emotional and mental energy. Our thought forms do not require a voice, a phone, or a direct connection. We direct them on a subtle energy level, targeting a reception point.

Often, as we have seen, our emotional energy spills over and with a jolt of mental energy leaves our subtle energy body going in no particular direction. Angry thoughts are like that. They just shoot out like wayward bullets in all directions, inflicting pain on innocent, unsuspecting people in their wake. But sometimes a spirit seems motivated to send a conscious thought to a specific target. Often the message is unspoken, even telepathic. Other times, the spirit drives home a message to a chosen target with great impact, even simulating a voice when there is really no physical voice left. It's a matter of thought power and thought control. Spirits often seem able to make you hear whatever they want you to hear in whatever way they want you to hear. Generally, the messages are specifically targeted to have that much impact.

It is also curious, don't you think, how ghost hunters seem able to record voices of spirits with audio recording equipment and even videotape images of spirits? I would just like to remind you that these spirits, be they ghosts or other nonphysical entities, do not have a physical form. They have no voice, no face, and no body. But the spirits seem able to make you hear and see whatever they want you to perceive. They can make you think you are speaking to your favorite aunt or your dead child. So, don't think a spirit can't make phone calls with a voice to impress you. From my former experience as a reluctant ghost hunter who was trained by a professional, I feel that ghosts can make you think that you are hearing a voice. This is thought control at work. In the dark work of strange messages from beyond, this is mind control. Spirits will reach out to you if you are receptive to their calls. Sometimes they have something important to say. Other times, they are just calling to complain. At times, they can be abusive. I do not recommend trying to initiate calls to the dead or any other spirits, since they need to move on. But at times, it's hard to avoid them when your phone keeps ringing at your home.

12

BRIGHTWOOD CALLS TO MISSING GIRL'S SISTER

Some of the strangest phone calls I ever heard about occurred on Mount Hood in Oregon in the 1980s. That is when I lived in Brightwood, halfway up that majestic peak. I didn't receive any of these calls, but one of my neighbors did. And they really freaked her out.

My neighbor lived just around the corner of our little development. I lived on a dead-end cul-de-sac, while she was on the main road that led into our half of the development on the south side of the Salmon River on Mount Hood. I had never met her until the summer day when she showed up at my front door with a secretary desk in tow. She had carried it the whole distance between our residences. She said too much had happened to her since she had moved to Brightwood and that she felt she should leave. She wondered whether I would like the desk. She said she designed and crafted it herself (I kept and used that desk for many years thereafter).

It was apparently a hard decision for her to leave, because she had moved up the mountain to try to find her sister. She and her sister were both from Portland, Oregon, down the mountain an hour by car. Her sister had moved to the mountain, leaving her behind in Portland, but then her sister sort of disappeared . . . The last thing her sister told her just before she disappeared was that she had discovered a cabin in the woods with some curious people who lived there. Apparently, my neighbor's sister was a bit mesmerized by the older women who lived at this mysterious cabin in the woods, and got to know them. My neighbor got the impression that her sister actually stayed with them awhile. From what she told me, her sister got the impression that the women who lived there were wise women, herbalists, and healers. The neighbor said her sister was troubled from situations and a relationship she had left behind in Portland. She found the old women in the cabin to be a comfort. And so they took her in. The girl really had nowhere else to turn, alone on the mountain and so far from home.

Here is where this story gets a bit murky. If not deadly, it certainly becomes dark. It was at this point that my neighbor lost track of her sister. So, she left her home in Portland to begin searching for her sister. She did not declare her lost. She figured she could just poke around in the area and ask a few people there. She should not be hard to find, she figured. But she was.

Both women were young. You might think that a young woman who stops strangers for help on a rural mountain would get plenty of support. You might also think that her young sister would attract a lot of attention in a rural setting, homeless and wandering. You would be wrong on both counts. Nobody my neighbor questioned seemed to know anything about her sister or remembered seeing her. And very few people she questioned wanted to say much about the healers in the log cabin at Sleepy Hollow. Either they did not want to talk, or they knew very little about the mysterious cabin in the woods.

My neighbor's search for her sister seemed to hit a dead end. She did find a person in Brightwood who gave her a place to live while she continued to search, but she was honestly about at the end of her search. She felt that her sister was alive. That is what she sensed, as sisters can often sense things about each other. So, she still didn't report her missing or get police involved.

Without much to go on, my neighbor settled into temporary housing around the corner from me. I didn't know her until that day she knocked on my door. She had been living there with a man I knew a little from dining at a mountain restaurant where he was a cook. I remember him fondly from his participation in our pioneer parade one summer in the town where my newspaper office was located. He dressed up like a bear to advertise the restaurant where he worked. He was a fine cook too.

I recall that he started dating a woman that I had once dated. As a result, we never became close friends, despite being neighbors a block or two apart in the middle of nowhere. Looking back, I could see where the woman who brought me her desk probably felt like a third wheel living there when my old girlfriend started showing up. She picked me to receive her handcrafted work because she had heard I once dated the woman her landlord now spent time with. It was a big mountain where we all lived, but a small community just the same.

When she knocked on my door, she explained exactly where she lived down the street in relation to me and how she knew about me. She explained that she planned to leave the mountain that very day and wanted to find a good home for the desk she had made. Before I could tell her how beautiful I found the desk and how impressive her carpentry skills were, she blurted out why she had come to the mountain and then why she was leaving.

A SERIES OF STRANGE PHONE CALLS

She had received a series of troubling phone calls at the house there. The voice on the phone sounded like her sister, although she could not determine the phone number of the caller. This seemed bizarre to my neighbor, because the phone at the house was not her own phone, but the phone of her landlord. My neighbor felt that her sister realistically had no way to know the phone number where she was staying, or even that she was on the mountain looking for her. It was unlikely she could even know the name of the man at the house. Still, the frantic voice of the woman on the phone sounded like her sister. Sisters seem to connect and recognize each other's intonations. They use words, phrasing, and expressions that connect between close siblings.

What is more telling, perhaps, is that the woman who called her knew her nickname as a child. She screamed out that she needed her help. But she provided little detail. My neighbor wondered whether her sister was trapped or imprisoned somewhere, but could not determine where she was exactly. When my neighbor asked questions of her mysterious caller, she got no response. The troubled woman just kept repeating that she was in danger and needed help urgently. It was as though nothing my neighbor said was getting back to the caller on the other end. I asked her at this point in her recitation to sit down and gather herself. I offered her a glass of water. We put the desk away.

My young neighbor wanted to unload her whole story, which she had somehow kept bottled up inside her during her time on the mountain. She had been looking so long and hard for her sister and asking anyone she thought might offer some kind of clue. She even moved into the area, hoping that being there would give her some insight to her sister's whereabouts. Then out of nowhere come these phone calls. There were a number of them in a short amount of time; each one seemed more desperate than the last. The familiar voice on the phone pleaded for help. There was an intimacy to the calls. The woman always called her by name and seemed to identify strongly with her. But never did she give any real clue as to where she was located or what kind of trouble she faced.

The last call my neighbor received at the Brightwood house was bone chilling, she said. As she told me about the screams and anguish on the other end, my neighbor became noticeably stiff and still. The color in her face changed. She was reliving a time she suspected was her sister's last gasps of life. And it sounded gruesome.

So, a few days later, my neighbor turned in her key at the house up the street and walked over to the only person she more or less knew anything about in our little development. She was expecting a ride back to Portland but figured there would not be room in the car for the desk. Or maybe she did not want the desk as a keepsake of her troubling time on Mount Hood.

I asked whether there was anything she would like me to do, but she just shook her head sadly. She seemed to feel that the situation was now hopeless, and the journey was ended. After she left me alone with her desk, I decided to poke around a little. I looked for any police reports that might sound like a young woman found somewhere or assisted. Usually, police blotters have a few words about just about everything and everyone found, escorted, rescued, detained, implicated, or suspicious. I found nothing. At least not initially.

CURIOSITY IN A SMALL MOUNTAIN TOWN

I kept thinking about the mysterious log cabin in the woods. I was working at the time as publisher of the community newspaper at the bottom of the mountain. The mystery of the women in the log cabin was intriguing to me as a journalist. I discussed it briefly with one or two of my newspaper staff members. They all lived at the bottom of the mountain so had nothing to offer. Nor did they have any clues or missing puzzle pieces. I wondered how intricate the pieces of this puzzle might be.

Perhaps the young woman had simply left the area after a few days. But it did seem odd that the women she described at the log cabin in the woods were reluctant to talk about her at all. And it still haunted me to recall the eerie phone calls my neighbor said she had received, the voice sounding trapped and desperate.

I would see these two older women, dressed in flowing purple gowns, walking in town. Nobody seemed to know them or even know anything about them. But they seemed to have an aura around them. They donated money to local charities. People knew that about them, but little else that they would tell me.

So, I dispatched a brave reporter to visit their log cabin in the woods, since he lived up the mountain too. He told them that he was interested in their healing work and wondered if they could help him. He begged off handling this story after his first and only visit to the cabin. Apparently, the old women who answered the door were reluctant to let him in. Eventually they did when he asked for their help as healers. My mountain reporter said he did not see a young woman or anyone other than the two older women at the cabin. He said that the women in the cabin frightened him with rough handling when they proceeded to give him what they called a healing. He said they told him to lie faceup on the floor. Then, he said, they lay their own bodies upon him and did things with their hands that were both painful and scary. The reporter said he could not wait to get out of there and never wanted to return.

I went looking for the cabin myself but was unable to gain entrance. The women seemed very guarded. I saw candles and herbs in the windows. They were reluctant to let me inside. I asked about the missing girl. They said they knew no such person and knew nothing about her whatsoever. So, I kept my eyes open and ears to the ground. Something out of place might soon offer a clue to these mysterious phone calls, I kept telling myself. It was just one more thing to think about on a community newspaper with constant deadlines and editions to be assembled. We had plenty to occupy ourselves at the paper at the bottom of the hill without spending time poking around up the mountain.

PUZZLE PIECES

Then some odd puzzle pieces surfaced on the mountain. We heard that the Welches Elementary School flagpole had been desecrated. Most alarmingly, it involved animal mutilation. Various birds in the area were slaughtered and hoisted up the flagpole where the Stars and Stripes would normally fly, except that it was summer, with the school in recess, so the flag had been removed for the season.

It seems that the patriotic firefighters of our Hoodland Volunteer Fire Department got involved too. They were outraged that one of the birds—the protected American bald eagle, was involved in the unseemly mess. Many people were angry, particularly with the bird that is our national symbol having been slaughtered and draped upside down up a pole beside the highway that connected everyone. People were insistent that authorities get to the bottom of this incident, to prevent such an incident from happening again and to properly punish the disgusting criminals. Some people suggested that it sounded like juvenile hijinks. But nobody shared any sort of clue.

This mystery continued without any other incidents for a couple of weeks and fruitless investigation, until something else caught everyone's attention. It was equally shocking to all, and perhaps even more threatening to life and limb. A body had washed ashore on a mountain lake. It was apparently mutilated, so identification was difficult. Also, it was badly decomposed. This became the new mountain mystery, but it really bothered people to think that they were now endangered. It had been a pretty live-and-let-live kind of quiet, rural setting—a getaway from urban problems.

A deputy sheriff from faraway Oregon City, at the other side of Clackamas County, came out to retrieve the body, once it was found. I wasn't there when he first came upon the corpse, since the call to the county sheriff's office about a dead body did not come across our police scanner. We pretty much focused on police and fire dispatches from our little town of Sandy, for the most part anyway. But I'm certain that a body retrieval call to Oregon City didn't set off any scanners. It was not an emergency situation—just a dead floater in a high mountain lake.

But floaters in our little lake were unheard of within the mountain community. Gossip spread across the hillside about the body being mutilated and unrecognizable. That's about all anyone talked about for a few days. I thought about the mutilated birds from a few weeks earlier, however, and considered a possible connection. Now, community newspaper journalists are not rocket scientists, but we do try to connect a few scattered dots at times. Mutilated birds plus one mutilated person seemed to add up to a troublesome source of dark cruelty. Especially when it all happened in one summer and geographically close. Added to the equation was the clandestine aspect to the crimes. Nobody seemed to want any credit. Nobody had left a calling card, insignia, or identification of any kind behind to claim credit for the superbad deeds. I always thought that such dark criminals would want some sort of token identification at the scene—not enough to positively identify them to authorities, but enough to satisfy their egos as a little signature that only they might identify. Not so, our perpetrators.

Then I thought about my neighbor's missing sister. Could she be the floater in the lake? My neighbor had found no clue to her sister's mysterious disappearance, since nobody remembered seeing her. There was only the sister's final report to my neighbor that she had found some interesting older ladies who lived in a cabin on the mountain and kept pretty much to themselves and their healing herbs. It occurred to me suddenly that nobody had run into this missing girl because she was floating facedown on a lonely lake for many weeks.

I have written about this little mystery in an earlier book titled *Conversations with a Reluctant Ghost Hunter: A Cautionary Tale of Encounters with Malevolent Entities and Other Disembodied Spirits*. Even when I return to this mountain mystery after so many years of reflection, however, I have little to offer in the way of a resolution or explanation.

The body in the lake was extremely hard to identify, and the county was slow to try to offer anything more after the deputy fished it out and brought it to town at the other end of our county. I tried to stay on top of the story, but the sheriff's department was reluctant to say anything since so little was clearly known. At last, they released the conclusion that the dead person in the lake was a young woman. I do not know whether that satisfied my former neighbor, but maybe it was a little bit of closure for her to end that sad chapter of her own life and move on without her sister.

No cause of death was firmly established, as far as I know. I think some residents on the mountain would like to think the girl had accidentally fallen into the lake and floated there so long that fish and birds had pecked away at her. Sometimes ignorance is bliss, I am told. I do know that the little log cabin where my neighbor's sister supposedly visited two herbalists suddenly caught fire one night. We never saw those interesting ladies from the cabin in town again. And, I hope, my former neighbor received no more disturbing phone calls from someone who sounded like her missing sister.

13

VISITS FROM DECEASED LOVED ONES AND PETS

Who among us has never sensed the lingering presence of a deceased loved one or a pet who has passed on? If you think back honestly with an open mind, you probably have too.

We are intimately connected to the people and the pets that lie beside us when we close our eyes to sleep and dream. So, it's easy to see how we feel their presence when they are near us in this way. When they are suddenly gone, you feel an immense void—almost as though part of you is gone. You feel a burning emptiness. This can be true of a loved one, a child, or even a beloved dog or cat. You try to feel that they are still with you in some sense, perhaps in your memory and in your heart. But the emptiness remains.

Then suddenly you sense that they are back with you somehow. How can that be? Many people have reported this phenomenon, and only psychics seem ready to offer an explanation. Still, you know what you feel. You can sense that missing loved one's return. Maybe you have other indications of the return as well. You smell them. The sense of smell is a powerful sense and often is associated with ghostly appearances. But the return of your loved one does not seem ghostly. You do not see them. You only smell them.

And then maybe you have the sense of touch. You sense that someone has somehow reached out and touched you, perhaps stroking your hair or touching your shoulder or hands—all sensitive areas. Maybe you heard something that could not be easily explained. If you are in a secluded, quiet room, it's often hard to explain such a sound, try as you will. A common report in such instances seems to be a mysterious indentation on your bed. There is a crevasse that suddenly appeared to disrupt the otherwise smoothness of your bedspread or a pillow that moments ago seemed untouched in this way. Many pet owners will remark that a beloved dog or cat that was reluctant to leave you even with death will seem to pounce upon your bed, just as you are settling in all alone. So, are you all alone? How do you explain a subtle bounce on your bed, as though a small creature had suddenly jumped up to join you?

THE RECENTLY DEPARTED

This sort of bedside mystery is most common, it would seem, shortly after the passing of a loved one who had shared your bed. In time, the smells and the pounce on the bed seem to disappear. It seems that the deceased need a little time to adjust before moving on. They had a routine, and you were an intimate part of it.

Some people will shrug off all of these suggestive clues, of course, refusing to believe that the deceased can return to us. Or maybe they find it a bit frightening. I would suggest that the recently departed might consider it their way to get one last hug or one last snuggle before their solo journey into the night.

Curiously, we tend to trust our five physical senses most of the time but often shrug them off at such times. And what about our sixth sense, our acute psychic sense to pick up on such things? Do we simply choose not to believe our own senses? Are we afraid to acknowledge that the ghost of someone so close to us has reached out to touch us one last time? I admit that the passing of a beloved pet has been softened on a couple of instances when my dear friend seemed to show up one last time at my bedside. Maybe my telling of their final return will jolt some similar memories in you.

MISS POLLY

My old cat, Miss Polly, showed up on my front porch years ago. She was a large female cat with a pearl necklace and probably too fat and old to have walked there on her own. In fact, she could not walk well at all, since she had been poorly declawed. I figured that someone had placed her there, knowing that I had cats and took decent care of them. I surmised that she had outlived her owner, who apparently fed her very well and sheltered her from much activity.

She was a Rose Point Siamese cat. When I asked her if she wanted to come inside, she just trudged up the stairs, flopped on the sofa, and started watching television. When I sat with her and started to go through the channels on my TV remote, she stopped me when I reached a daytime soap opera. She especially seemed to like *General Hospital*. So, I always kind of felt that Miss Polly had belonged to an old lady who sat around on a sofa, watching daytime soaps and eating chocolates.

When I took her to a veterinarian to see if she was healthy, the doctor asked whether I realized how old she was. She was at least fourteen, he said. Well, Miss Polly was to live many more years, reaching approximately twenty-one years of age before throat cancer caught up with her. We banned smoking in the house shortly after Miss Polly showed up, and should have done so sooner. Perhaps her former owner smoked too, imprisoning the couch-bound, fat cat in a room filled with stale smoke. You know, the little lungs on a cat or dog in your home are just as sensitive to secondhand smoke as that of a young toddler.

Anyway, I did not learn about her cancer until I took her to the veterinarian for dental work. He tried to treat the cancer, but it was already spreading. She was already around twenty-one at that time. Polly would try to prop herself up in her weakening position to continue, as though nothing was wrong with her physically, but she was fading more with each new day. She would struggle to climb onto my bed. I had a couple of other cats who would wait patiently for her to join us. She would eventually find her way on board, making a big indentation when she finally pulled herself up by her claws and fell down on the bed.

The night she died was unusual, to say the least. Miss Polly tried to climb into the bed but dropped backward and went limp. She seemed to die there on the spot. I checked her lungs and felt for a pulse. I could see no sign that she was alive. So, I pulled her up into bed with the other two cats and me. I petted her and gave her a loving goodbye. I kissed her on the head. I propped her up to spend the rest of the night with us, planning on a dreaded morning burial in the gardens that she loved. The other two cats filed by her, also kissing her on the head. I have noted that ritual of respect among cats. Then we just sat there looking at our dearly departed friend.

That is when Miss Polly surprised us. With a jolt, she raised her head from the dead and swiveled it around to face me, eyes wide open. Then she collapsed once more on the bed, never to rise again. My two remaining cats held a vigil over her body that night. After we buried Miss Polly in the garden near the garage, they often visited her in the late morning or early afternoon, almost like a ritual.

GEORGIE

Years later, another cat appeared on my front porch, apparently homeless like Miss Polly. Aside from his current condition, he was entirely different from my old cat with the pearl necklace. He was a striking tabby and looked young and healthy. He was bright orange with white stripes and appeared to have a little Manx in him. Neighbors indicated that he had been hanging around the neighborhood for some time and once was rescued by workers at a business on the next block after he was hit by a car. Since nobody there felt that they could give him a proper home, they released him back on the street after his cast was removed.

After days of hanging around on my front porch, I started to feed him. He was pretty shy from being so long on his own, but eventually he came indoors and became my best friend. But there was a severe price that my new cat Georgie had to pay for living his first year and a half on the streets. He had not been inoculated against common diseases and tested positive for feline leukemia. He became a close companion and comfortable coming into the house through a cat flap in the back of the house. A gentler, sweeter, and smarter cat never graced my acquaintance. He seemed to know instinctively when I would be coming home and exactly where my car would appear, because he was always curbside waiting for me whenever I pulled around any corner to park my car.

I knew his life would likely be shortened by the feline leukemia. At the age of eight, his health deteriorated sharply. Rather than let him suffer from a certain death, I took him to his veterinarian for humane euthanasia. He continued to purr as the shot put him into a deep sleep, his eyes focused on me, filled with my image. I could see my reflection in his eyes, even when he stopped breathing, patiently awaiting the end. The last thing I said to him was that his death that day was only an end to his physical suffering and that it was not the end of him. He was a very smart cat and seemed to listen.

After Georgie's passing, I would hear what sounded like a cat enter my bedroom and climb up on the back of an easy chair beside my bed. I had become accustomed to hearing this sound, since I had heard it many nights before. Georgie would spend part of his nights slipping into my room to hop up on the big chair to perch on the backrest. There he would sit and watch me sleep. It was a specific sound the way he used to slip through the cat flap to my bedroom door and jump onto the back of my recliner. I have had other cats in this bedroom, but the sounds of Georgie entering the room were different. His movements were swift and deliberate.

On nights shortly after his passing, I would smell him in the room and sense his gaze upon me. Then after a few days, these mysterious visits seemed to disappear. I suspect he missed me and wanted to say goodbye a little longer before moving along. But he was a swift and deliberate cat, a smart cat that knew his life had not really ended.

THE PET WHISPERER

I know that the grieving process for many people who have lost beloved pets can last an exceptionally long time. I used to moderate a popular podcast called *Healing with Your Pet: Our Psychic, Spiritual Connection*, with many of our episodes still posted here and there online. Some of the most replayed shows we did for the show involved pet loss. People with a strong bond to their pets often have trouble moving on without them. They just will not let them go. I would have guests on the show to recommend a book of memories with pictures and other keepsakes to celebrate their lives. Other guests would discuss pet grave markers or memorials. One of our most beloved shows seemed to be when I slowly read the poem "A Rainbow Bridge," which discusses the happy playground where former pets might find themselves upon passing.

Some people, however, seem to want more. They seek to contact their deceased pets. I do not recommend that but recognize that it often happens. There is this small window when the dead often reach out to touch their loved ones for a final time together. The window seems to be the same for our pets as for our human friends and relatives who reach out to us. Usually, this will happen in the week after a physical death. More precisely, it seems to happen within three days of passing. After that time, the spirit seems to move on, as it should. It is a long journey, and our brief stop here is just one leg of life's journey, most likely. So, don't be surprised if your cat or dog seems to curl on your bed one last night after passing. They are just saying goodbye. The contact is their own choosing.

My concern is when people try to keep their beloved pets attached to them, even after they have passed. Your obedient, loving pet will often oblige. That means they cannot move on. That strikes me as selfish on the part of the grieving pet owner. Some special pet whisperers even claim the ability to connect you with your deceased pet for final closure. If done soon after death, this probably is not such a bad thing. I have done it myself. When a cat that I rescued off the street had trouble coexisting with my other pets and I was unable to relocate her in a suitable home nearby, I found a farmer in a neighboring state who welcomed getting another barn cat. I figured that might be the best place for Buttons. So, I drove many miles one early day to relocate her with a farmer who claimed to have a special relationship with cats. The farmer promised to care for her and feed her in his country setting. I regretted moving Buttons, and she howled the whole way.

I was soon to understand her apprehension. The farmer let her roam, and Buttons was hit by a tractor on a quiet dirt road at the farm. She had not been there long, and I felt guilty for the choice I had made in placing her there. I felt a deep urge to tell her how sorry I was and to assure myself that she had somehow moved on all right. She had a hard life and a terrible ending to it. Speaking to her one last time might help both of us find closure. My problem was that I was not anywhere near the farm where she had died. Also, I had no experience contacting dead pets. I had studied pet communication and become fairly acquainted with telepathic communication with pets in the conventional sense. But this was beyond anything I had been trained to do or ever tried before.

So, I thought of my friend, a former coworker who had moved away and started a psychic service where she would contact deceased pets for grieving owners. I heard she was good at it, and felt that she was someone I trusted. So, I gave her a call. I told my friend truly little about Buttons. I gave her the cat's name and the fact that she had died on a farm shortly after I relocated her there. My friend thought that was enough for her to make contact. She called me back with a surprising amount of detail about my relationship with the cat and the life of the cat—things I had not told her. She told me that Buttons had a lot to relay to me. She said Buttons had been my cat many times before in previous lives and would return to me again, if I found her better living arrangements. She said that she was no longer upset with me. She said that she had lived with me many times before, sometimes as a dog and even once as a rabbit. According to my friend, Buttons told her that she returned to watch over me as a companion and often intercepted cancer to protect me (I do remember many pets who have died of cancer). Then Buttons apparently told my friend something remarkable that she wanted me to hear. She wanted me to know that our pets can be light-bringers too, with a special life mission to come to earth and spread light. Buttons said that she was one such light-bringer.

TV PSYCHICS

Today there are many psychics who claim this ability to contact our dead pets and connect us with them. I have met only one—my former coworker whom we just talked about. But you have probably seen or heard of others. We have even seen one or two on television, demonstrating in front of cameras and a studio audience an apparent ability to contact our dead pets. The one I remember best was a woman who would walk up to people in her studio audience and tell them about their dead dog or cat sitting next to them. Then she would proceed to tell these people what their former pet wanted to say to them and how they would always be with them. This is not limited to psychics who offer to help us speak to our beloved pets who have died. I have even seen a man on television who offers to connect people to their deceased friends and relatives. In convincing fashion, he walks among a studio audience and sits with guests who have lost loved ones they wish to contact. He chats with these studio guests for a while and then offers to channel special messages from their deceased friends, reaching out to them wherever they might be today. You might have seen him on television or in one of his many appearances across the country. He is quite famous. What I notice is that the dead will readily return to speak to you only if they want to speak to you. And I always worry that people try to force that, drawing loved ones back here to a life they have left behind and should leave behind.

14

GHOSTS IN HOUSES

Some people seem to notice ghosts, while many others do not. Years ago, I worked with an experienced ghost hunter who showed me that it was really all about learning to listen. Since this book is essentially about learning to listen to become more receptive to hidden voices, I think my teacher's words might prove helpful here.

First of all, my teacher would not want to be identified as a ghost hunter. She did not hunt them in an aggressive manner. She did not stalk them, confront them, and seek to destroy them. In that sense, she was not a hunter. No, she would identify herself as a communicator, one who learned to listen well. Nothing I say about my teacher could do her justice as someone who bravely went into houses to work with ghosts. How I came to meet her and become her student is an amazing story in itself. I had never planned to hone any sort of skills for communicating with ghosts or working in haunted buildings. One day, however, I visited the psychic author Louis Gittner at his inn on the island where he lived. Like a lot of people who visited him there and studied his books, I considered him my teacher and advisor and returned to his island regularly to meet with him. His special ability to channel hidden voices of spirits around him has been well documented in the classic book by Brad Steiger, *Words from the Source: A Metaphysical Anthology of Readings from the Louis Foundation.*

When I asked for Louis at the front desk, I waited in the dining room for him to appear. Instead, a woman came out to meet with me. She introduced herself only as Helen and explained that she worked with Louis as his assistant. She said that Louis had asked her to spend some time with me in his place. She said she did not know exactly why Louis had said that, since neither of us had received any additional prompts from Mr. Gittner.

She began to tell me how she visited houses where people had asked for help with hauntings. She wondered if knowing something about that sort of activity appealed to me personally and whether it was anything that I wanted to learn. Admittedly, I had seen a ghost or other spirit form previously without any real training. It occurred to me, therefore, that I might be a natural to learn what she did when she visited haunted houses.

When I told her that I was interested in her work and asked her to continue, she hesitated for a moment. Then she asked me whether I was sure. When I answered that it was all right, she told me that what I chose to do with any of the information she would provide was entirely up to me and that I could use it to do the sort of work she did or not. She proceeded to tell me how people would contact her through word-of-mouth referrals when they suspected that their house was haunted. She kept a low profile and didn't advertise or seek publicity. It was a service she provided for the ghosts as much as the people whose houses they apparently haunted. She told me that some people die and fail to fully move on in a natural way, because they are either afraid of what they would find if they moved on or because they were reluctant to leave this physical world. Sometimes they clung to places and people and would not let go, she suggested, and other times they didn't fully realize that they were physically dead, or they were in a state of denial.

These were the ghosts she claimed she could help, but only if she could make meaningful contact with them. She would sit and wait for them to contact her and make themselves known. She learned to get into a receptive state through heightened awareness. She would sit very quietly, tune out all external and internal distractions, and patiently wait to hear something. Sometimes they would appear before her. Other times, she would simply hear them inside her head. She would not attempt to banish them but instead would try to comfort them and assure them that she would try to help them in their confused state. She would suggest to them that they had no further business here in the physical world and needed to move on for their own sake.

Part of them had already moved on, but their emotional body and lower mental body would sometimes remain with their lower personality, which tends to cling to its identity and surroundings. So, she would attempt to console them and then convince them that they had reached a time of transition with nothing left for them here in their past, but a future for them when they fully moved on. My new teacher was not so much religious or spiritual as she was practical and empathetic. She would sit with them. Her ghosts often would appear wearing a coat and hat, perhaps carrying an umbrella or cane, she said. It was apparent to her on many occasions that the spirit of the deceased person knew enough to prepare for a journey but was reluctant to take the final steps from this world. So, she would assure them that these final steps were natural and their best course of action, with nothing significant left for them here. She would convince them that the living did not really observe them or interactive with them in any meaningful way, and that the places they haunted were now properly reserved for the living. She said that once she listened to them, recognized them, and related to them, then the spirits of deceased people who haunted houses would generally go on their own without a struggle. The same would be true of pets who had trouble leaving their homes and owners.

OTHER FORMS IN THE SHADOWS

There were other instances, she suggested to me, when hauntings were not simply deceased people who were reluctant to leave. Sometimes the spirits were not the ghosts of deceased people and were not so easily handled by a concerned outside person such as herself.

She said that people sometimes thought their homes were haunted, but she found no ghosts whatsoever. The spirits that inhabited the dark corners of these houses were sometimes emotional bodies that had been created and fed by the strong, negative emotions of people who lived there. These powerful thought forms of emotions and mental energy that spilled out of occupants at the house eventually took the shape of people as shadowy, dark forms that resembled their creators. These were forms of raw, negative emotion that were scattered throughout the building. She claimed that she thought it particularly sad when she found one of these dark emotional bodies in some corner of the building. It was always difficult for her to tell the residents of the house that the form would continue to grow with repeated emotional outbursts and would shrink only when no longer strengthened by additional negative thought forms. These are runaway thought forms at their worst.

Sometimes it is hard to continue living in such a home, if the source of these negative thought forms was not the current occupants, but earlier residents. The only hope might be to starve the negative thought form being, in hopes that it would shrink and disappear. As forms that have no reasoning ability, it is hard to believe that they would plan any sort of relocation or rehabilitation on their own.

I asked my instructor on ghosts what to do about the spirits of deceased people or other intelligent entities that might not agree to leave willingly and needed additional persuasion. She suggested a few tried-and-true tools that people often carry when dealing with ghosts. I'm not certain that I remember her list of tools perfectly after all these years, but I can give you the list of things I remember bringing with me on my own investigations. Whenever people would call me to investigate their haunted house, I would generally take some kosher salt, spikes to drive into the ground on the four corners of the building, and a hammer to drive the spikes. I would generally bring water too, although holy water would probably have been the right choice. At times, I would also bring a mirror to try to catch the spirit in the mirror or show it that it had no form and did not belong on this physical plane.

My feeling from talking to the ghost expert was that she helped a great many people with her ability to listen and communicate with spirits in their homes. She helped many ghosts of deceased people move on willingly, abandoning the earthly homes where a shell of their former existence hung on for dear life.

Not everyone who seeks to remove unwanted spirits from buildings is as fortunate or helpful as my teacher, as I later learned. In my case, I left her after a long weekend of instruction with answers to everything I could think to ask about this shadowy process. Unfortunately, I could not foresee the problems that I would later encounter when good friends would ask for my help when they stumbled into a haunted place.

I simply told my teacher upon parting that I had no interest in her sort of work but was nonetheless grateful for the information she offered, in the off chance that someone would later need my assistance with a haunting. I could not predict then what difficulties I might encounter down the road when pressed to apply what I had learned in that brief time.

Seeing or hearing a thing—even on a subtle level where we see with new eyes and hear with new ears—cannot fully prepare us for dealing with the unknown. It only allows us to perceive what is otherwise not obvious to our physical senses. Noticing ghosts as I had done since I was a child is one thing, while actually knowing what to do or how to respond to them is quite another. So, when my teacher asked me about my previous experience with ghosts, the question did not surprise me or upset me. I see them all the time. The difference is that prior to my training in ghost communication with her, I simply observed them and moved on, not even acknowledging their presence or thinking much about it. Talking about ghosts that I have seen did not seem like a good topic to bring up with friends and relatives. They tended to think I was basically sane and saw and heard only the obvious physical things that everyone else noticed and felt comfortable talking about.

UNCOOPERATIVE SPIRITS

My first request from a friend to investigate a ghost did not involve a haunted house, but a haunted church. Parishioners at this church in Portland, Oregon, had long agreed that it appeared haunted by some sort of spirit, and that troubled many of them. There are probably lots of haunted churches, from what I have heard, but I figured that a ghost in an old church was probably a former clergy member or longtime church member who clung to the church through some sense of devotion or emotional attachment. This cleansing did not seem terribly hard to me at the outset. If the ghost was seen regularly by many people over the years, I assumed that I could make contact easily and would find it not terribly shy about communicating with a willing contact such as myself. Boy, was I wrong!

Everything that could possibly go wrong on an attempt to "de-ghost" a building happened on this day. I thought that going there on a quiet Saturday afternoon and getting dropped off by a friend would give me ample opportunity to contact and communicate with the ghost and ask it to move on. My friend from work was familiar with the church and drove me there in our newspaper's old Buick. He let me in, as I recall. Or maybe the church was not securely locked. It was so long ago that memories fade.

Anyway, I entered the dark, old church with a gym bag that contained my tools, should the ghost need a little persuasion. I moved from room to room but noticed nothing unusual. I would sit in a room and try entering a meditative state so that I would be attentive and ready to pick up on something. Finding nothing in many rooms, I eventually found my way to the basement. I figured that's where a ghost might hang out.

Finally, I noticed a sound and sat very still, trying to establish contact. It was the heavy footprints of someone walking. After a while, I peeked down the way and caught sight of what looked like a custodian walking away. I worked my way up to the top of the building and sat in the balcony above the sanctuary. I sat in the absolute stillness of the darkened area without picking up on anything. Then I noticed what looked like a flickering light in a corner of the sanctuary below. When I reached that area, the flickering stopped. So, I began to leave. Just then, a small light turned on. It was in the area that I had just vacated. Then it switched off. Was someone or something playing with me?

Exiting the sanctuary, I found myself in a dark hallway. Everything was deadly quiet. I stood there, wondering what to do next. Suddenly, a loud thud made me jump. I tried to place the sound, which seemed familiar. It occurred to me that it might be the sound of a heavy door closing. I thought about the custodian leaving the church and locking the front door behind him.

I rushed to the door and found it impossible to open from the inside with no key. Hmm. Now what? I wandered around a bit on the lower level of the church. Then I heard another sound—a different sound. In the basement kitchen area, I found a window that was a little ajar and rocking back and forth in the wind. That seemed to explain my mysterious sound. I drew a glass of water and tried to think about how to leave through that upper window. I returned with a chair from another room and found that I could just fit through the window, if I tossed my gym bag of tools out ahead of me. Careful to leave without breaking the window, I fell onto the hard parking lot.

Back at the Buick, my friend wanted to know if I had gotten rid of the ghost. I had to tell him that I had not made contact and had been pretty unsuccessful. I asked him to wait a few minutes longer, while I walked around the outside of the building. It was time to put the tools in the gym bag to good use. If the ghost there would not cooperate, maybe I could flush it out.

I sprinkled a thin, unbroken line of kosher salt around the entire building. Then I took out my four spikes to drive into the four cardinal points of the building. I called on the four angels to protect the building from unwanted spirits. I did a brief banishing spell to drive the spirit from the building. Back in the Buick with my friend from work, I looked back at the old church one last time, as we rounded the corner to leave. I do believe I caught sight of a little light that flickered in an upper room. Was it playing with me?

A HAUNTED TRAILER IN THE WOODS

I should have quit offering to help friends with ghost problems right then and there. But then some friends who lived in the national forest on Mount Hood begged me to check out their haunted mobile home near Rhododendron. Their story was compelling.

An herbalist friend, her daughter, and her husband lived in someone's single-wide trailer without paying rent in exchange for keeping an eye on things. There was a shed out back with carefully marked canning preserves, which were abandoned for some reason. There was also a large tree outside with the names of various dogs and dates beside the dogs. Both features of the property were mysteries to the three people who lived there with their own little dog, who roamed the surrounding woods freely.

The herbalist told me that her daughter reported seeing a little girl with golden curls inside a trailer, as sort of an imaginary playmate that nobody else saw. The herbalist also told me that some invisible force or spirit had tried to strangle her and her husband in their sleep in the back end of the trailer. She said the trailer seemed haunted, and asked me to do whatever I could to remove any spirits I might find there.

On the night I visited to try to establish contact with a spirit in the trailer, I asked the family to wait outside on the front porch. I sat on the girl's bed in the front of the trailer and tried to make contact. I got very still and tried to listen. I sensed something was there but also sensed that any spirit there was guarded and unwilling to communicate or be seen. So I got off the bed and walked through the trailer, passing a narrow hallway where I had to squeeze past a washing machine and dryer. I looked in the back bedroom where the herbalist and her husband claimed some invisible spirit had grabbed them by the neck in their sleep. On the return trip through the dark hallway, I was startled by what I saw.

I clairvoyantly saw a dark, angular figure sitting on the dryer. It looked at me in a menacing manner, disgust in its red eyes. With a jolt, I responded. "You are no little girl with blond curls!" I blurted out. It just looked at me with utter contempt and then disappeared in front of me.

I returned to the front bedroom and sat there for a while, trying to think what to do next. I felt that I needed to connect somehow with that creature and try to remove it if I could. It also seemed to me that we were not dealing with the ghost of a deceased person, but some other spirit entirely—a shape-shifter. Looking into my back of tricks, I pulled out my latest addition—a mirror. I called to the spirit and tried to get it to present itself again. I teased the spirit that it could use the mirror to see itself. I suggested that seeing itself in the mirror would make the spirit whole and a part of this physical world.

When I felt the presence of the spirit upon me, I rushed to the door and smashed the mirror on the front porch, stomping on the glass. I suggested to the herbalist and her family that the spirit was probably out of their house now. That was certainly my hope.

I'd like to think that I salted the trailer and placed the spikes at the four cardinal points around their home to banish the system from their home, but I know that I was frantic and more concerned with my own safety. All I really remember well from that night is that I got into my little car to drive back down the mountain.

In my car, however, I felt something grabbing my neck and choking me. I drove back to the trailer. I'm not proud to say it, but I returned with the spirit in my car. The next night, I followed fire trucks up the mountain to the trailer in the woods. The trailer had suddenly caught fire. Nobody could determine how or why. The family's little dog was found burned under the trailer, apparently chained to the trailer in a way it had never been restrained before. This was a mystery.

Sometimes spirits do not want to communicate with us. A few spirits out there are malevolent and should be avoided. We probably should walk around these troublesome spirits and keep our distance at all cost.

15

OUR NEWSPAPER GHOST

Most ghosts are simply deceased people who are reluctant, afraid, or too confused to fully move on. They are not harmful. In fact, they tend to be shy and reclusive. They will let themselves be known from time to time, to establish their presence. But they do not want to come face to face with anyone. They offer us just a fleeting glimmer out of the corner of one eye, if you look carefully enough. They are hiding in the shadows, living out a ritualistic pattern of behavior as the shell of a person who now possesses only a fading image of a former personality, a few early emotional connections, and limited remaining mental faculties.

That certainly fits the ghost at our newspaper plant in Gresham, Oregon. I don't know if he's still there, but I doubt if he would move on as long as that building remains. He seems to feel that he belongs there and always has.

I met him years ago when our mountain paper was printed there. I would visit the plant after-hours to drop off material and sometimes finished work there. It was generally quite late at night. Typically, I would work on final layouts in the break room, where all the snack machines were located. There was a door to that small room, separating it from the front office, editorial offices, advertising offices, composition room, camera room, and pressroom. It was quiet in there almost any time of the day, but especially quiet at night when all the other people were gone and all the lights were turned off. At times, I would use one of the computers to enter some new copy into the plant's main drive. It always felt a little odd yet pleasantly tranquil to work there after-hours with no distractions. One night, however, I noticed several distractions, but not from anybody that I knew or could see there. They were phantom sounds that rocked me inside out. I'm not certain that they were physical sounds, but certainly something that I heard distinctly inside my head.

I was working at one of the snack tables in the room with the vending machines. The door to the rest of the plant was closed. My light in that snack room was the only one in the building, to my knowledge. From inside the break room, however, I heard a loud thud. I assumed that it came from an area toward the back of the building, in the composing room. I wondered who it could be so late at night. I had found the place locked when I entered the building and locked it again once I was inside. Only a very few people had keyed access to the plant after-hours.

I opened the door from the lunchroom and put my head around the corner to the right, where the composing room, camera room, and pressrooms were located in back. I saw and heard nothing. So, I looked to the left at the editorial area, the advertising section, and the front office. No lights, no sound. "Hello?" I shouted into the void. No response. Only stillness and darkness.

So, I returned to my table and half cup of coffee in the lunchroom, closing the door behind me. And I worked in peace for another half hour or so. Suddenly a very loud sound broke the silence all around me. I tried to determine what could make such a loud sound. It was a puzzle. Then I thought of the very heavy doors between the composing room and the pressroom in back. I had noticed that those heavy doors required a lot of strength to open. After someone walked through them, the doors closed with a very heavy thud.

POWER TO OPEN HEAVY DOORS

There seemed to be a lot of air pressure in the pressroom. Maybe that created the pressure on the heavy doors. It was important to shield the rest of the building from the roar of the presses on the other side of those doors. Yes, I decided. These heavy doors create the sound that I had just heard. But how could that be? It would require a strong person to open those doors. It could not be simply a draft. The newspaper plant was built like a bomb shelter, very sturdy and made of concrete. The areas were isolated and soundproofed to a degree by heavy doors between sections. Some people in the building needed relative quiet to think and work, while presses created a thunderous sound that required press operators to wear protective headgear in the back.

So, I concluded that somebody had to be in that building with me to open such a heavy door or otherwise create so much noise heard throughout the entire plant. Very gingerly, then, I snuck into the composing area and looked around. I saw nothing there. I peeked into the window of the heavy pressroom doors behind the composing area. I could see nothing in the dark. It was all that I could do to steel my nerves to open the door just a crack and wedge a foot into the heavy doorway that led to the presses. I peered around the doorway and listened carefully. It was perfectly still and without any activity or motion. It was very dark back there, and I saw nothing like a light that someone would need to operate back there.

Remaining still, I patiently waited for something to break the stillness with any kind of clue. I sensed nothing whatsoever back there. So, I allowed the door to shut as slowly as possible to avoid sound. I turned my attention to the composing room again. I walked from area to area. I saw nothing. But I did not feel alone there. I sensed a presence. I was rather familiar with every inch of that composing area, since I spent most of the day every Wednesday making up our weekly newspaper there. The large room had several typesetting stations and light tables at an angle, large tables for assembling pages and large ads. The room was normally dim, so that the light tables were most effective.

The room this evening was very dark with no lights in the building. It was absolutely still. I inched my way from area to area, examining everything carefully to see if there was any life or any sign that anyone had recently been there. I found nothing. Nonetheless, I could not shake the feeling that someone or something was present with me there in that large room. I noticed the mirrors in various corners of the building, but they held nothing as an indication that something was behind me and out of my line of vision.

As I began to walk through the composing-room doors into the editorial area, I felt very conscious of attention on me. I did not look back. Instead, I steadied myself and got into a heightened state of awareness to try to sense what was there—to see with new eyes. I was able to restrain my fear long enough to reach a still point and a blankness deep within me, a place of receptivity not filled with emotions and thoughts racing through my system and clogging my mind.

SEEING WITHOUT EYES

Very clearly, a picture formed inside the empty screen before my mind's eye. It formed instantly, fully constructed and detailed. It was the image of a hunched-over, old man in dark work clothes with a green visor on his head. He was seated in a chair in front of one of the composing machines. I had never seen such a man, except in old photographs. He looked like one of those old-time typesetters who used to sit in front of hot-lead Linotype machines to compose the type for early newspapers. It occurred to me that this might be a newspaper ghost, an early compositor from a bygone era who felt compelled to remain in a newspaper printing plant forever, doing the sort of work that once occupied him and consumed his life.

I collected myself and then turned around, half expecting to see him sitting there. I did not. If he were there, he seemed oblivious to me and everything outside his never-ending work on the night shift. But I still felt a presence, the way you will sense another life form in your midst. Back in the lunchroom, I hurried to finish my work. I was almost ready to leave when I heard another odd sound from outside the lunchroom door. It sounded like the keys of a typewriter being struck. There was a rhythm to it, as though operated by someone who knew how to type very well. I opened the lunchroom door, just as the last keys were struck. The sound carried easily throughout the empty building. It sounded as though the typewriter sound had come from the very front of the building, in front of the editorial department. That is where the office staff worked near the building's front doors. Now, this really intrigued me. I started to walk up to the front of the building, where the typewriters were stationed for the front office staff. The rest of the building's staff used computerized word processors, but the older women in the front office seemed to prefer the use of a typewriter for much of their work. It seemed to me that the machine I had heard sounded like a manual typewriter and not an electric model.

I focused on a couple of older machines up there but saw no one and heard nothing more. So, I turned around and left. I gathered my things and left the plant. I thought I had heard enough for one night. I locked the building securely, after glancing around once more to see that all lights were off. They always were. Whoever had slammed those heavy doors and typed on the machines did not seem to need lights. I was glad to go.

I tried to clear it from my mind. I felt guilty that I had not tried to make any effort to connect to the spirit and communicate. Maybe it was a ghost of an old newspaper employee who did not realize that he no longer worked there. Maybe it was someone who refused to believe that he had died, or was afraid to move on. Helen, my ghost-hunting teacher, would have tried to help him. I did not, and I am not proud of that. Later that night, tossing and turning in bed, unable to sleep, I kicked myself for not checking what the spirit might have typed on the machine at least. I considered that it was doing it in ritual fashion without much regard to what message the selected keys he struck might say. But it probably did say something. The typing had a smooth flow of keys being struck, as though by someone who knew how to type and was actually spelling out words and sentences.

Of course, there did not seem to be any paper in any of the typewriters that I saw in the front of the building. So there would not be any record of what was typed. It was not until much later that I learned you could check the rubber rollers on those old manual typewriters and see what keys had been struck. Maybe a ghost of an earlier newspaper staff was actually trying to communicate with me. Unfortunately, I was not receptive to the message at that time.

ANOTHER EXPLANATION

As the summer there wore on, I did begin to formulate another possible explanation. I did know someone at the printing plant who had died. It was someone who had recently worked there at nights and could very well be the ghost who haunted our printing plant. I did not think of her back then, because I didn't know she had recently died at the time. In fact, I was under the false assumption that she was very much alive and still working at the newspaper plant. In truth, this young woman had left her employment there, and people had sort of lost contact with her. She had worked there only a short time as a part-time employee and worked pretty much alone, after normal hours.

She hailed from Texas and applied for a job as a compositor. She mostly set the type on advertisements, back in the old cut-and-paste days of cold type composed on photo-sensitive receiving paper. It was state of the art then, and a big step up from the hot-lead type of Linotype days, but a predecessor to the more computerized ways printed pages are now more easily assembled.

I met her only a couple of times, since she began her shift there just about when I would usually drop things off at the end of a normal workday. She would sit at the largest typesetting machine we had. That is the machine that was normally used to set the type for the big advertisements that included a full range of type styles and sizes. A person had to be a rather good typesetter to work this machine. The compositor had to be able to look at a rough layout and select the fonts and size of letters that would match the layout. Very select people were given this assignment.

She had just come up to Oregon from the Lone Star State with friends and landed this job after just a little training on the big machine. She worked alone at night so had to catch on fast. She seemed to like working there. I remember speaking to her once in the lunchroom just before she started her night shift. She was cheerful and delighted to be there. What I did not know was that her time there was short. She was helping friends test a new boat on the Columbia River, in the gorge, and died in a freak accident. The big boat was out for a test of a new steering system of some sort, which apparently malfunctioned. The power boat tried to make an abrupt 360-degree turn in the middle of the swift river. It immediately capsized with her inside the cabin below. She was trapped in the turned-over boat, as it filled with water inside the cabin. She drowned in the accident. Death probably came slowly, as she fought for air.

It occurred to me that my young friend, the night compositor, might have been the newspaper ghost. Part of her might want to be back there in the safety of that concrete plant, working alone in the middle of the night. But then, that didn't explain the clear image I received of the old, hunched-over man with the green visor. He seemed more likely to haunt the place than the young woman. I say this in part because the ghost of the newspaper plant seemed to be acting out some sort of repetitive tasks there, like a spirit trapped in some sort of time loop. The spirit did not seem to respond to me.

RITUAL PATTERNS OF GHOSTS LOST IN TIME

Ghosts who are unlikely to connect with you in any way or seem unwilling to communicate often go through the same activity in one place in a sort of ritual performance, seemingly oblivious to physical life around them. They will typically appear in the same way at the same time of day. It's almost as though they were performers with a matinee or evening performance. Sadly, they are apparently stuck in a sort of time loop, where they live out the same scenes of significance to them. They seem to have no realistic sense of the time of day or the conditions around them. It's almost as though they are walking in their sleep. They become part of the landscape.

Maybe Helen could help them connect and communicate with them, so that they could move on. But these spirits are not even observant of the people or activities around them. You could try to hook up equipment to record their utterances and catch their essence on film, but you would likely be disappointed. They tend to say the same things over and over and flitter about in the same manner each day. If they materialize at all, they tend to appear in the same place at the same time of day. Consequently, it is pretty difficult to communicate with them, since they do not recognize you as a receiver and do not listen to you if you try to send them a message. They seem to act as though they are performing the same scene over and over in an empty theater, since they do not recognize any audience or respond to audience reaction.

People on Mount Hood used to comment that they would catch what looked like early-day pioneers resting beside broken-down wagons on the old Barlow Trail, where I lived. These were fleeting images, but always the same and always frozen in time, oblivious to the present-day activity around them. I once saw what looked like a band of dark-clothed pioneers walking out of an old barn. The image was like a scene out of time.

They carried crude farm tools. I saw them at dusk out of the corner of one eye, as I was pulling into town at the bottom of our mountain one late-spring day around dusk.

I stared at them exiting the old barn. Then, just as soon as the farmers had appeared, they quickly disappeared in front of my eyes. It was like watching a very old movie whose film was fading. I mentioned this odd sight to a couple of psychic friends in town. They said they had noticed it too. In every instance, every one of us had seen them walking out of that old barn at dust, carrying early-day farm tools. Who knows? Nobody was ever able to verify the sighting. But we all saw the same scene reenacted. Never did any of the ghosts who exited the barn wave at us or seem to notice cars racing past them.

16

THE ORDER LEAVES THEIR MARK IN AN ATTIC

I do not believe I ever encountered ghosts or any other spirits who tried harder to communicate with me than the mysterious spirits at my house on Laurel Avenue. My mysterious squatters actually spelled it out and embedded their words in stone. They kept repeating their message until I listened and responded appropriately.

They were good at hiding too. I lived in that house three years before I even noticed them. And that was only because I had finally moved into the secluded part of the house they occupied. You see, they lived in the attic on the third floor, an area that was basically ignored except for storage for many years. The house in the historic district of old Saint Paul was built in 1900. It had Doric columns in front—white pillars to complement the white house. The house had a first-floor fireplace that was intended for use with coal. The first and second floors had beautiful oak flooring, the dark and narrow boards that you see only on older houses these days. The common living space of the house was on the first floor. That is where we had the formal dining room with wainscoting and a lovely oak cabinet with mirror. The first floor also included the living room and foyer, which had the same dark oak flooring. The bedrooms on the second floor had oak flooring too. It was clear that previous owners of the house had focused on the first and second floors.

Leading to the third floor was a rare rosewood stairway that had been painted over with a dull-blue paint for some odd reason. The winding stairs to the third floor led to attic space, which had been remodeled over the years to include one bedroom and two spare rooms. The hallway flooring on the third floor consisted of crudely painted rough boards, pale blue to match the odd stairs. The hallway on the third floor was dimly lit by a wall lamp in the middle of the hall. The bedroom to the left faced the front street, with curious little cubie holes and doors that led into a dark crawl space. Since this bedroom was rented to a housemate, I kept checking the crawl space on both sides of the room and putting out rodent bait just in case rodents were somewhere inside there. The space was creepy. Originally, I lived alone with my cats in this three-story, turn-of-the-twentieth-century house. Subsequently, I placed an advertisement to attract housemates. I found that I had a lot of bedrooms to rent once I began reviewing the unused, extra rooms more closely.

The previous owner had been a banker who stayed in our city less than a year before she was transferred to another bank in another state. I noticed that she had turned many of the rooms into hobby centers. There was an exercise room, a sewing room, and a room for her antiques. There were so many bedrooms that she did not really have much use for. So, when I moved there, filling up the many bedrooms with housemates, the new occupants started using the added rooms for storage. That was certainly true of most of that dreary third floor.

The third-floor bedroom that faced Laurel Avenue had a narrow passageway into another smaller room that previous occupants apparently used as a sort of sitting room or reading-room annex to the bedroom. The first thing I did when I started renting bedrooms to roommates was to seal off the passageway to make a separate bedroom of the smaller room. The third room at the far end of the third floor was pretty much just attic space used for deep storage. But eventually one of my roommates saw it as a larger bedroom, rough as it was. Almost everyone in the house got involved in a rehab project to make this rough attic space a proper bedroom. It had a lot of nooks and crannies, as attics often do, but was not that comfortable when we first started work on it. I went down to a local carpet store and found some carpeting and carpet pad on sale. I learned to lay carpet while working in that attic. And when I finished, the large space had wall-to-wall green carpet. It was beginning to look livable. But the big fireplace extension from the first floor jutted through the room. And there was nothing like a closet.

I noted that the attic just opened into crawl space and rafters on three sides of the room. I plugged the crawl space in the middle of the room by installing a small trap door. I plugged the crawl space in the far corner of the room with a permanent enclosure, since it was a very small opening. I converted the other crawl space opening into a deep closet and installed bars to hang clothes there. So, with the open closet that I created, the crawl space remained completely open and uncovered in one part of the room.

The new bedroom overlooked the backyard, which had been paved to create a parking lot. It had a large, white window frame and four window panels within the frame. Since we were entering warmer months, when we needed an air conditioner more than four little windows in this upper room, I removed the window frame to make way for a wall unit to cool the place. I stored the window frame in the crawl space in the back of the newly created closet for easy retrieval in the fall. The bricks from the fireplace extension were something I figured I did not need to worry about. The red bricks looked just about the way they probably looked when installed in 1900. The fireplace had to extend through the house somewhere to reach the ceiling, and the attic seemed the logical place to run it, no doubt. After I painted the walls and installed the carpet with help from my roommates, I came upstairs to pick up my things and clean the room. I stood back and had to admire the nice bedroom that we had created out of the extra space.

MYSTERIOUS GRAFFITI

Then something odd caught my eye. It was on the fireplace bricks. I suddenly noticed something appeared to be written on the bricks in black letters. Why hadn't I seen that earlier? Was it always there? Since the house was built a century earlier, a lot of people had access to the attic over the years. On the other hand, it was probably the least visited room in the entire house, used only for deep storage. Or that's what I thought, anyway. I had been there only a couple of years out of the last century.

I got up close to read the letters directly in front of me. The inscription struck me as a bit cryptic. It read THE ORDER. The almost perfectly proportioned letters were approximately an inch and a half tall and looked like they had been written with a black marker. The letters did not seem so perfectly formed that they had been done with a stencil. They looked drawn by hand. Wondering how I might have missed them on the side of the brick wall just to the left of the door by the entry, I had to scratch my head. No, they were not bold black but appeared a little faded. They didn't jump out at you, unless you were looking squarely at them. They were at eye level.

The inscription should have been obvious to all of my housemates who entered that room numerous times in recent days. Some of the tenants there had entered the room on other occasions to store and retrieve items. So, if it was an old message that had faded over time, people in the house had ample opportunity to notice it. As I learned in talking to my roommates, nobody had. They said they had never noticed any words written on the side of the fireplace extension.

In any regard, I figured that I could remove the inscription from the bricks and be done with it. So, I gathered a bucket, scrub brush, and some concentrated cleaner. I scrubbed for some time until I felt that you could no longer see more than a very faint impression of the original black letters. The message was not totally erased, but pretty much muted to where you could barely see anything there. So, I was satisfied that THE ORDER was gone.

Was I in for a surprise! The next day, I returned to do some wall touch-up and thought to look at the fireplace extension as I entered the room. Shockingly, the black type with the words THE ORDER was there again. It looked just the way it had looked before I cleaned it.

I considered that the letters were not written with something like a black marker but were etched into the bricks somehow, with the impression impregnated deeper into the stone facing. For the first time, it occurred to me that this was not some old message and that it was not delivered in a conventional way. That made me wonder who or what could have printed this message so impressively onto our brick wall. I also began to seriously wonder at that point just what the message meant. Was THE ORDER a thing or a group? With the type reappearing, it almost seemed like the source of this message was protective of the words. So it was beginning to occur to me that THE ORDER was a group. It could be a personal statement of identity and belonging for the originators of the message. Was some group trying to establish territory there in the room in the way street gangs will sometimes mark public buildings or streets with personalized graffiti to claim their place there? I wasn't ready to accept that idea so readily. It was possible, I figured, that I had failed to properly remove the inscription from the brick fireplace facing. After all, if the words were etched into the bricks, I would have to scratch below the surface of the bricks to remove this graffiti. Most certainly, I did not want to alarm any of my housemates with any concerns that I might have at that point. I wanted to just get rid of the message on the wall and forget the whole thing.

So I got some steel wool and sandpaper and tried to remove the words from the bricks again, digging deeper this time. I decided that I probably needed to put a little elbow grease into the project to get it done right. I scrubbed with the steel wool and sandpaper until the bricks were filed down to where they had lost some of their red color. Finally, I was confident that the letters were no longer visible. The next day, however, the black letters were visible again, as though I had never tried to remove them. I began to wonder if someone was sneaking into the room and reprinting the letters in black each new day. It would be quite a practical joke. I didn't consider my housemates to be practical jokers, but what other earthly explanation did I have?

ELIMINATING THE OBVIOUS

So I locked the room that day, confident that nobody else had a key to the room that had been opened and unlocked until that day. I felt certain that was the end of the story, one way or another. Just to make certain, I came up to the new bedroom the next day to check. The room was still locked, so I felt certain that nobody had entered it (it was a deadbolt lock and would have been hard to hack from the outside). Amazingly, the black letters again appeared on the brick fireplace wall, just as during my previous two inspections. I remarked that they looked exactly the same. They were in the same place and looked identical in size to the earlier letters. That made me feel, once again, that the black letters were embedded deeper into the bricks than I had earlier believed. The letters always looked the same, so maybe I was failing to really remove them. So, I got a chisel and began cutting deeper into the brick to remove the black letters. I kept checking, so that I did not cut more into the red bricks than necessary. At last, I felt that the letters were gone. There was no trace of them whatsoever.

Confident that the message was properly removed this time, I smiled as I cleaned up the filings on the new carpet and put my tools away. I locked the room again. I began to feel that removing the message was a little like sweeping the whole thing under the rug, however, since I had no clue who had written the message, why they had written the message, or what it meant. But this seemed to be attaching too much concern to the mystery, since I would probably never get to the bottom of things, really. The best I could do was to clean the room for someone to occupy.

Toward that end, I returned the next day to determine that the room was still locked and things were orderly for a new occupant. The black letters, however, appeared on the brick facing again, as though defying my efforts to remove them. So it occurred to me at last that the message was indeed a statement of defiance. Something called THE ORDER wanted to establish claim to the space that had never been occupied, and had marked their identity in stone. But who or what was THE ORDER? And why would they protect their claim to the space? Many mysteries, with few clues.

So I decided to try to communicate with them, if they were somewhere up there in the attic, guarding their presence and yet trying to hide. Part of me still clung to the impression that the inscription was some old remnant that was simply hard to remove, despite the fact that nobody in our house had ever noticed it before. But what did I have to lose in reaching out to whatever entities might be up there in the attic? I could try to make contact, but how would I know if anyone was really there?

"Hello?" I called out softly. "I know that you are here. I see who you are. I read what you wrote."

I waited for a response. I sat in perfect stillness, waiting for a response that never came. I was starting to feel pretty foolish. But I persisted.

MAKING CONTACT

Walking over to the big open area of the crawl space, beyond the newly formed closet, I turned my head around the corner and stared into a vast expanse of dark rafter space. I saw nothing. But I did feel a presence. Maybe it was just my heart beating hard. I don't know. But I continued.

"You don't have to worry about us," I said. "We won't bother you. We can work this out. You cannot occupy any part of this room, because it is now a bedroom. This room belongs to the living. It belongs to the physical person who will live in this new room.

"But you can remain up here in the attic, if you want. Only, you must remain deeply hidden in the crawl space beyond this open room. If you do not disturb this space, nobody will disturb you in the crawl space. You are welcome to stay there."

Still, I heard no response and saw nothing. Oh well, I figured. Nothing ventured, nothing gained. I left the room, locking it again. When I returned the very next day, however, the black lettering on the bricks was muted. It was only a faint image that a person would have to look hard to distinguish. I never saw any sort of graffiti appear on any of the walls there again, which was good with someone moving into the room.

I would occasionally ask tenants who stayed in that room whether they had noticed anything unusual in the room or seen anything out of sort. Nobody ever did. Nobody ever complained about staying in the room. In fact, it seemed to be a peaceful place that people enjoyed as a bedroom. I might add, however, that I discouraged all renters from storing anything in the deep crawl space or going into the crawl space. I offered basement storage instead. Between renters, I would clean out the room and occasionally paint it and shampoo the carpeting. I would look for anything odd, particularly in the crawl space. There was never anything odd.

I sold the house a few years ago after owning it for seventeen years. At that time, I spoke to my renter who had occupied it for many years, right up to move-out date with the sale of the house. He said that he and his elderly cat found the room to be very warm and cozy. I asked him point-blank, since the house was now sold, whether he ever felt like the house was haunted in any way. He shook his head side to side with a little disbelief.

The only thing I found a little odd after the black graffiti on the brick facing disappeared, however, was the disappearance of the window frame. I had removed it and placed it in the crawl space. I never found it again and had to create another window. For several years I searched for the window frame and never found even a clue of what had happened to it. It remains a mystery. Maybe THE ORDER knows.

17

FRIENDLY GHOSTS IN QUEEN'S HOUSE

Not all spirits who bump into us in dark places are shy and reclusive. Take, for example, my house on Van Buren Avenue. When I was in the process of selling my old house down the street in Saint Paul, I took my dog Nikki on her favorite walk to a nearby park. She loved to roll on her back in the tall grass there and wander through the trees. On the way back one day, she stopped in front of a white house on a corner. It had a nice, rolling hill with tall grass. Nikki started rolling in the lawn there and did not want to leave.

I noticed that it had a for-sale sign in front, something that I had not noticed before. I scheduled a tour of the house, largely because Nikki liked it there so much. I figured the steep stairs inside would detour her, but the old dog with hip dysplasia and spondylosis dashed up and down the steep stairs to the second floor like a young puppy. So while it needed a lot of improvements and was clearly overpriced, I bought the house, nonetheless. I was soon to learn it held some surprises.

I did not do much to change the interior of the turn-of-the-twentieth-century classic. I did stain the original oak fixtures in the great room. Curiously, they had been painted over with some icky white paint. I also resurfaced the narrow and dark oak flooring in the great room, an elongated living room with a fireplace at one end and a large arched window at the other end. I repainted all walls and cabinets in the kitchen. But I really didn't do much to the interior, most of which was original construction—except for a back-bedroom extension.

I painted the exterior, added a new front walk, repaired some stairs, stained the front porch, and added guardrails both on the side and front steps from the street. But those were pretty much cosmetic changes. The house remained basically the way it was built back in 1900, like my previous house in town. I guess you could say that I am a sucker for period architecture. The house was one of the two oldest homes in that neighborhood. The house across the street on Aldine was built about the same time.

PLACE WITH A LOT OF HISTORY

In fact, the alley behind that house across the street was a remnant of a historic pioneer trail that once led from the city of Saint Cloud all the way to the river docks on the Mississippi in the Twin Cities. I could tell some of its history from the existing abstract for the old property. The rest I learned from neighbors who had lived in the area for generations and knew some really exciting stories about the place.

The builder of my new house was apparently a Jewish businessman who also built the houses on either side of mine. In fact, two of the houses still shared a common garage. The story was that the Jewish gentleman used to work at a desk in front of the huge, arched window at one end of the great hall in my new house. The window probably had an amazing view to the east at one time, when there were few houses there. But now it faced only the house built to the east and looked into the living room of one of the two houses that the gentleman added to his row of houses. Another story of the house that intrigued me was that the British rock band Queen once lived in my Van Buren house for about six months in the mid-1970s, when their drummer was recovering from an illness. The neighbors who had lived there for many generations liked to talk about the outside going-away party the band hosted for the neighborhood. Apparently, it went into the wee hours of the morning. That was when the band was trying to get recognized in the United States, and just before they made it big. Apparently, their lead singer went ahead to the West Coast to try to land a good record deal, leaving the rest of the band at the corner of Van Buren and Aldine in Saint Paul.

I was able to verify this story through a disc jockey who personally knows one of the remaining members of the band. This band member remembered the house and neighborhood when I sent him photos. I got an email confirmation forwarded to me through the disc jockey. Yes, the place looked very familiar, according to the response, even after so many years.

It was also apparent from the more than one hundred years of records contained in the abstract for the property that the house had been through a lot. Strangely, though, not everyone stayed long. When I moved there with my sick cat and dog, I didn't think much about what vibes might come with the house. The roof didn't leak, and the heat worked. All the windows opened. I was fine with the house, except for one or two odd things that I noticed over time.

Even though I was preoccupied at the time with my sick pets, both of whom were old and dying, I did seem to sense another presence in the master bedroom, where the three of us huddled together. I didn't sense that in any other part of the house, really. It didn't seem to me to be a creepy bedroom or dreary in any way. In fact, it was warm and cozy. My bedroom was a large extension to the house and had wall-to-wall carpeting. It had windows on three sides. The walk-in closet by the door was huge. And recessed ceiling lighting was like something you might see in an old movie theater.

WET SPOT THAT WOULD NOT GO AWAY

I had my bed in the back of the room, by the windows on the east side of the house. Later I moved it more to the center of the room, near the center windows, but discontinued that when I started to notice a wet spot near the bed on the west side of the room. At first, I thought that one of my elderly pets was incontinent and causing the wet carpet problem. But the cat always used the litter box, and the dog waited to be let into the yard each morning before relieving itself. Moreover, the wet spot didn't smell anything like urine. It didn't have much of any smell that I could recognize.

So I would dry the wet spot each morning and then hope for the best. But I would find the same wet spot in the identical spot each morning. I devised what I thought was a foolproof plan to get to the bottom of things, so to speak. I put a can in the place where the wet spot always appeared, thinking that it must be a roof leak of some sort. But each morning the can was empty.

I tried peeling back the carpet to see if something from beneath was oozing out of the ground each night. I found nothing wet under the carpet.

I tried putting dry rags on the windowsills to see if somehow there was some water seepage from the windows. Each day, however, I would find the rags to be dry.

No, the only wet spot was that little section of the carpet, a mystery that I never resolved. So I just learned to live with it. I mean, I had much more on my mind at the time. I simply kept my bed and other things away from the wet spot and dried it whenever I thought about it. There were few of us in the house at that time, since I had just moved there. Nonetheless, we did lock our bedroom doors during the day and during sleeping hours. Nobody else in the house seemed to know anything about my bedroom's wet spot or seemed to be in a position to enter the room to cause mischief.

NEW EYES ON THE PROBLEM

In time, I moved out and rented out the entire house to various tenants. So there was somebody new in the master bedroom that my sick cat and dog once occupied. I didn't mention the wet spot, probably because I had sort of put it out of my mind. And it didn't bother the next occupants, who always seemed to place their bed, dresser, or television over the wet spot. Nobody ever mentioned anything odd about the carpet.

Most of the occupants who followed me in that room, however, stayed for a short time for some reason or another. That was until Daniel ("Rusty") Blackmore moved there in 2009. Besides being my renter, I also knew him as a fellow Theosophist and part of the international Theosophical Society. He lived six years in the same room that I once occupied at the Van Buren house, and got to know it better than anyone else, perhaps. Rusty noticed many odd things about the room over time and was willing to share his impressions freely for this report.

Rusty started seeing ghosts in that bedroom. He told me that he had experienced ghosts before, but his encounters at the Van Buren house were different. He said it was like a personal relationship – one that lasted in part far beyond his stay at that house. Rusty said he didn't notice either of the two spirits in the house prior to 2012, when they first revealed themselves to him in that master bedroom.

"It wasn't a haunting," he said. "It was a presence. The first ghost that appeared to me looked like an older gentleman. He wore a dark suit of clothes and a large hat that was dark also."

Rusty said the clothes looked like something from the turn of the last century. He also said that the man's appearance with his odd hat and clothes reminded him of "an old Hasidic Jew." Rusty explained that he would catch a glimpse of him out of the corner of one eye. Only once did the old gentleman look at him directly.

"He was owning that space," Rusty said of him. "He seemed to belong there. He never went through the door but entered the room only when a door was open. He would slip in and out of the room. He revealed himself, though, like he wanted me to know he was there. But he didn't seem to want to communicate."

Rusty said that these apparent ghost sightings happened almost entirely in the back bedroom at the old part of the room. That part of the room seemed to be part of the original construction and not the extension. There was a large closet there by the door, which was where the sightings usually occurred. Rusty then began to notice another entity in the room, which he identified as more of a disembodied spirit without form. He said he could not initially determine much about this one, because it had no structure like a person or recognizable clothes. Initially, it appeared to him like a cloud. It remained at the closet at the entrance to the bedroom where the older gentleman was most often seen.

"You could see that area of the room like an energy field," Rusty said. "It was an area that was rich with energy and at the same time dark, almost like a cloud."

GETTING CLOSE AND PERSONAL

Then one day the dark, formless energy field appeared at Rusty's bedside. That very first night, he addressed the formless energy. "It's all right," he said. He told the spirit that he was not afraid of it. For the next five or six visits, the energy field would appear off to the side of his bed, looking at him. He said that it would then hover over his bed, with him in it.

"It was amazing," Rusty said. "I asked permission to put my hand up into the energy field. There was a sort of blue-gray ethereal emission. I asked if I could feel it. I would hold my arm up above me for a minute or two—as long as I could—and that blue energy started forming around my hand like a glove. It was sort of tingling. It was not radiating, but illuminating. Before that night, it had appeared only like a dark cloud that moved slowly."

After a while, Rusty said that he started talking to both of the spirits. "You're there again," he would tell them. "You don't have to be afraid," he assured them.

He said that the formless energy field eventually revealed a face. He said that it was the face of a young lady perhaps twenty-two to twenty-five years old. The first two or three times she appeared in this manner over his bed, Rusty said he thanked her. He said she seemed to smile at him.

"Whenever this force revealed itself," Rusty said, "it was benevolent. It radiated with happiness. I seemed in no way threatened. She seemed to want to let me know that she was happy I was there. It was very comforting and good."

These were not lost spirits, he said of the two entities in his room. He insists they were just letting him know that they were there. Nothing in the room ever shook or rattled. There was never any sound. The spirits never in any way appeared harmful or frightening to him.

"It was like I was being checked up on," Rusty said. He said that he saw the old gentleman outside the back bedroom only once. Rusty explained that he was sitting in the long great room at the end with the fireplace. He saw the old gentleman slip from around the hallway that separated the great room from the back-bedroom closet area. Once the ghost was noticed, Rusty said, the old gentleman would always slip away.

One night when the lights were out, Rusty said he noticed the area by the closet to be especially dark. That was the only time the old gentleman faced him directly and stared at him.

CONTINUING VISITS

Curiously, the visits from at least one of the spirits of the old Van Buren Avenue house seemed to continue after Rusty left the home. About three years after he had left Minnesota, the young woman appeared in his new apartment on Quincy Street in Rapid City, South Dakota. He said that he didn't ask it to follow him, and he didn't call it in any way. It just appeared, he said. It came to him one night in bed at a time when he felt relaxed.

"One or two times there," he said, "I experienced that same blue-gray emission and held my hand into the bioluminescence. It happened the same way. It was dark, and then it was light. She appeared to me, and I said, 'Oh, it's you again!' I didn't see her face there, only the same light. It was like her telling me, 'I'm checking up on you.'"

Rusty said the ghosts of Van Buren Avenue seemed to be happy there. He had no impression, he said, that they were in any way unhappy. "That is a place they knew very well and felt comfortable," he said of the old house in Saint Paul. Since leaving his apartment Rapid City, Rusty said he has not heard from his spirit friend with the blue-gray light.

Neither Rusty nor I ever heard other residents of the house speak of ghostly encounters of any sort while we lived there. It must be said, however, that our encounters with mysterious messages from beyond happened there in an area pretty much confined to the back-bedroom extension. Other people who occupied that bedroom during the years I owned the building stayed briefly, without comment on wet spots, costumed gentlemen, or blue energy fields. In comparing notes with Rusty over what I had read and heard from neighbors about the history of the house and his own ghostly observations, we both feel that the old gentleman Rusty saw from time to time was the Jewish businessman who had built and occupied it. We figure that he still felt at home in front of the arched window, where he used to spend his day working. When he would slip into the back bedroom, Rusty recalled, he seemed to be slipping around the corner from that direction.

Theosophical study by Rusty made him think of the spirits at the Van Buren house as beings who had died and separated the silver cord that connects our physical life with our high self. The life essence or higher self leaves the physical world upon death when the cord is separated. With some people, elements of their physical presence might remain with aspects of their personality, emotional body, and memories of the lower mind. Maybe part of them refuses to leave, is confused by their physical passing, or else feels a strong attachment to a place or people here.

In organizing this old house on Van Buren Avenue, I decided at one point to position a little table and a couple of chairs in front of the large, arched windows at one end of the great room. It just felt comfortable and felt right. Maybe the old gentleman who once lived there and worked at a table in front of that big window appreciated it too. Who knows?

I sold the house a few years ago to a group of investors who planned to extensively remodel the old house. I hope they do not disturb our old friends in the back-bedroom extension. My feeling is that they will not change the back bedroom, because it is a nice master bedroom near a full bathroom and the kitchen. And I don't see why they would change the beautiful arched window where the original owner reportedly worked day after day. It's part of a great room with lovely antique floors, oak built-in woodwork, and a pleasant fireplace area.

Mysterious messages from beyond can be nonverbal. They can be as simple as body language, a warm glow, or a smile. They can be delivered by conscious thought forms that require no outward sound whatsoever.

18

CONSCIOUSNESS EXISTS EVERYWHERE ON ALL LEVELS

We need to revise our common idea about what constitutes communication. We tend to think of messages that we send and receive as words spoken within earshot or delivered through some mechanical relay. We tend to recognize communication as something between two physical beings. Sufficient evidence shows us, however, that communication needn't be verbal or even reliant on our five physical senses.

Some whales deliver clear messages across vast oceans. Their focused vibrations successfully target other whales across the globe. We can bridge huge gaps too, if we learn to really listen and project our thoughts.

Hearing thoughts does not necessarily require ears. In fact, thoughts can be projected without any sound. The only question is whether you can receive the thought form. Many people have experienced some sort of telepathy. Maybe you just knew someone was thinking of you or just knew that someone was planning to call or visit. Similarly, we can see without using our eyes, if we can pick up on the thought form being imprinted on our consciousness. We all possess consciousness to greater and lesser degrees. The only question is whether we can learn to efficiently use it.

We use our consciousness both to send thought forms and to receive thought forms. Expanding our consciousness and learning to heighten our consciousness would appear to be key in learning to communicate more fully. Consciousness is awareness within a life form. It is not unique to human beings. There is a certain level of conscious awareness in all living things. Life itself is consciousness, according to ancient Eastern spiritual science.

The ancient wisdom tradition has long spoken of the driving force behind all of creation and the transitions that it brings to human consciousness. Ancient wisdom holds that the universe was created and exists through consciousness or infinite mind. It maintains that the universal consciousness upholds all of creation. *The Secret Doctrine* views the absolute reality behind all of creation as consciousness. That is the underlying primal intelligence. H. P. Blavatsky's book based on ancient insights gathered in the Himalayan hideaway of adept spiritual masters describes how cosmic consciousness as spirit manifests in the form of nature all around us. Her source, the *Book of Dzyan*, sees consciousness as fundamental to cosmic evolution on the grandest of scales. The ancient mystic authors of this book, considered the world's oldest manuscript, saw consciousness in all things, from nature to living beings and the cosmos itself. These ancients saw consciousness as constantly expanding and evolving.

In examining the consciousness within us, we must admit that it is a driving force outside the physical realm. When we are asleep, we creatively dream. In our waking, vivid dreams, we experience out-of-body experiences. When tranquilized in a hospital operating room and no longer processing analytical thought, we nonetheless experience conscious thought freely. Even the dead seem to experience consciousness, as we have learned from many documented cases of near-death experience where the dead are returned to life to tell their amazing stories of out-of-body consciousness. We can see that our consciousness, as a part of spirit, exists outside our physical bodies on all subtle energy body levels. It is a part of the energy vortex that surrounds our physical form, existing on an emotional body level, a mental body level, a causal body level, and on our higher body levels as well. It is our spirit. As such, it is part of our eternal life force or everlasting energy. It connects us to all of life, which also operates on a consciousness level. Maybe we should call it life awareness. In our higher state of heightened consciousness, we are extremely aware and extremely adept at communicating to every living thing around us.

There are many things heightened consciousness can do for us. We can project thought forms more efficiently to manifest real changes in the life around us. That, of course, is when we send thought forms. When we learn to use our consciousness more efficiently to receive thought forms, we can become better listeners.

THE MANY SPIRITS SPEAKING TO US

What could we hear with these new ears? There is a vast cosmos of things we can hear. We can hear the projected thoughts of loved ones across the world. If we become good receivers, we can receive thought forms from spirits from everywhere. We can hear nature spirits, angels, and even the voice of God, if we really learn to listen. We can hear the thoughts of ghosts and spirits from other dimensions. We can even hear voices from the past and voices from the future, since spirits are not limited by our physical limitations of time and space. We can hear the voices of the lost and the suffering who call out for help. We can hear the symphony of the universe. The possibilities are endless.

That leaves us with the sad admission that most of us are so disassociated and remote that we live our lives like people lost at sea who are clutching the top of a vast, bobbing iceberg. We are unable to discern the vast ocean of voices that surrounds us or the infinite expanse of space above us. There is so much that we do not hear or see, as we sit precariously balanced on the peak of a drifting iceberg. The position in which we place ourselves, of course, is a product of our own making. We choose to put ourselves in this position, rather than listen to the voices around us and see the faces who call out to us with their thoughts.

Thought forms as consciousness energy travel at light speed. They can go anywhere and reach any designated target. They could scatter in all directions to touch many lives, or effectively reach a focused target with full impact. We could be that viable target. It is up to the target, however, to become a willing receiver.

WE MUST LEARN TO LISTEN.

SO MUCH DEPENDS ON IT.

AFTERWORD

As a journalist with a metaphysical interest in expanding consciousness, I have tried to tell the stories of mysterious messages in this book as accurately as possible. If you have not personally experienced what we might consider hidden voices or messages from beyond, then you might reasonably question the validity of these accounts. I would hasten to add, however, that this is my truth and the truth of the people I have interviewed. My truth is not necessarily your truth, since you have not personally experienced it and have no frame of reference.

Rest assured, however, that you can experience voices from beyond yourself, if you really learn to listen on a deeper level of heightened consciousness. Early chapters in this book offer personal exercises that should help you develop new ears for hearing and new eyes for seeing. I don't personally claim to have special psychic gifts, nor do most of the people described in this book. We just acquired ability to hear what others might overlook. In my case, I had excellent teachers.

While I have tried to tell the stories in this book as honestly and fairly as possible, I recognize that the case I make for mysterious messages from beyond is based on purely anecdotal evidence that is not statistically conclusive or scientific. These are stories with impact for the people who lived them. Maybe they will ring true for you as well.

Effort was made throughout this book to mask the identity of most of the people described in these stories. I believe that both the dead and the living are entitled to privacy. Some of the people in this book requested that I shield their identities. Everyone in this book, however, freely provided information to share and worked with me to guarantee detailed accuracy. You can consider every story in this book to be true, according to the people who are described in these stories.

Von Braschler

BIBLIOGRAPHY

Amao, Albert. *Awaken the Power Within: In Defense of Self-Help.* New York: TarcherPerigee, 2018.

Amao, Albert. *The Birth of a New Consciousness and the Cycles of Time.* Bloomington, IN: Authorhouse, 2016.

Arkani-Hamed, Nima, Savas Dimopoulous, and Georgi Dvali. "The Universe's Unseen Dimensions." *Scientific American* 283, no. 2 (August 2000): 62–69.

Arntz, William, Betty Chasse, and Mark Vicente. *What the Bleep Do We Know?* DVD. Los Angeles: 20th Century Fox, 2005.

Aurobindo, Sri. *The Secret of the Veda.* Pondicherry, India: Sri Aurobindo Ashram, 1971.

Backster, Cleve. *Primary Perception: Biocommunication with Plants, Living Foods, and Human Cells.* Anza, CA: White Rose Millennium, 2003.

Bailey, Alice. *The Light of the Soul.* New York: Lucis, 1955.

Bailey, Alice. *A Treatise on White Magic.* New York: Lucis, 1998.

Barbour, Julian. *The End of Time: The Next Revolution in Physics.* New York: Oxford University Press, 2001.

Bartusiak, Marcia. *Einstein's Unfinished Symphony: Listening to the Sounds of Space-Time.* New York: Berkeley Books, 2003.

Bell, Madison Smartt. *Lavoisier in the Year One: The Birth of a New Science in an Age of Revolution.* New York: W. W. Norton, 2006.

Bentov, Itzhak. *Stalking the Wild Pendulum: On the Mechanics of Consciousness.* Rochester, VT: Destiny Books, 1998.

Besant, Annie. *The Bhagavad Gita: The Lord's Song.* Adyar, India: Theosophical Publishing House, 1953.

Besant, Annie. *Thought Power: In Control and Culture*. Wheaton, IL: Quest Books, 1967.

Besant, Annie, and Charles W. Leadbeater. *Thought-Forms*. Adyar, India: Theosophical Society, 1901.

Blavatsky, Helena P. *Collected Writings*. Adyar, India: Theosophical Publishing House, 1966.

Blavatsky, Helena P. *The Secret Doctrine*. Adyar, India: Theosophical Society, 1986.

Blavatsky, Helena P. *The Stanzas of Dzyan*. Andesite, 2015.

Blavatsky, Helena P. *The Voice of the Silence: Chosen Fragments from the Book of the Golden Precepts*. Chicago: Theosophy Company, 1928.

Bowman, Carol. *Children's Past Lives: How Past Memories Affect Your Child*. New York: Bantam, 1998.

Braschler, Von. *Confessions of a Reluctant Ghost Hunter*. Rochester, VT: Destiny Books, 2014.

Braschler, Von. *Moving in the Light*. Pine Mountain Club, CA: Shanti, 2018.

Brennan, Barbara Ann. *Hands of Light: A Guide to Healing through the Human Energy Field*. New York: Bantam Doubleday Dell, 1988.

Bryant, Edwin F. *The Yoga Sutras of Patanjali*. New York: North Point, 2009.

Campbell, Don. *The Roar of Silence: healing Powers of Breath, Tone & Chant*. Wheaton, IL: Theosophical Publishing House, 1989.

Castañeda, Carlos. *Journey to Ixtland*. New York: Washington Square, 1991.

Castañeda, Carlos. *A Separate Reality*. New York: Pocket Books, 1991.

Castañeda, Carlos. *Tales of Power*. New York: Pocket Books, 1991.

Cooper, Callum E. *Telephone Calls from the Dead*. Hampshire, UK: Tricorn Books, 2013.

Dossey, Larry. *Healing Words: The Power of Prayer and the Practice of Medicine*. New York: HarperCollins, 1993.

Dushkova, Zinovia. *The Secret Book of Dzyan: Unveiling the Hidden Truth about the Oldest Manuscript in the World and Its Divine Authors*. Moscow: Radiant Books, 2018.

Einstein, Albert. *The Theory of Relativity & Other Essays*. New York: MJF Books, 1955.

Emoto, Masaru. *The Hidden Messages in Water*. New York: Atria Books, 2005.

Emoto, Masaru. *Messages from Water and the Universe*. Carlsbad, CA: Hay House, 2010.

Emoto, Masaru. *The Miracle of Water*. New York: Atria Books, 2007.

Gawain, Shakti. *Creative Visualization*. San Rafael, CA: New World Library, 1978.

Gittner, Louis. *Listen, Listen, Listen*. Orcas Island, WA: Louis Foundation, 1980.

Gittner, Louis. *Love Is a Verb*. Eastsound, WA: Louis Foundation, 1987.

Godwin, Joscelyn. *Harmonies of Heaven and Earth: The Spiritual Dimensions of Music*. Rochester, VT: Inner Traditions, 1987.

Goet, J. Richard. *Time Travel in Einstein's Universe: The Physical Possibilities of Travel through Time*. New York: Mariner Books, 2002.

Grierson, Francis. *Psycho-Phone Messages*. Amazon Digital Services, 2011.

Hall, William J., and Jimmy Petonito. *Phantom Messages: Chilling Phone Calls, Letters, Emails, and Texts from Unknown Realms*. Newburyport, MA: Disinformation Books, 2018.

Heline, Corinne. *The Esoteric Music of Richard Wagner*. La Canada, CA: New Age Press, 1974.

Hirshfield, Alan. *The Electric Life of Michael Faraday*. New York: Walker 2006.

Hodson, Geoffrey. *Basic Theosophy*. Wheaton, IL: Quest Books, 1981.

Hodson, Geoffrey. *The Call to the Heights*. Wheaton, IL: Quest Books, 1975.

Holy Bible, King James Version. Peabody, MA: Christian Arts Publishers, 2013.

Joseph, Frank. *Our Dolphin Ancestors: Keepers of Lost Knowledge and Healing Wisdom*. Rochester, VT: Bear, 2016.

Joseph, Frank. *Synchronicity as Mystical Experience: Applying Coincidence in Your Life*. Pine Mountain Club, CA: Shanti, 2018.

Karagulla, Shafica, and Dora Van Gelder Kunz. *The Chakras and the Human Energy Fields*. Wheaton, IL: Theosophical Publishing House, 1998.

Koontz, Dean. *Mr. Murder: A Thriller*. New York: Berkley Books, 2006.

Krishnamurti, Jiddu. *At the Feet of the Master*. Lulu.com, 2018.

Krishnamurti, Jiddu. *Commentaries on Living*. Wheaton, IL: Theosophical Publishing House, 1995.

Leadbeater, Charles W. *The Chakras*. Wheaton, IL: Theosophical Publishing House, 1997.

Leadbeater, Charles W. *A Textbook on Theosophy*. Adyar, India: Theosophical Publishing House, 1962.

Leek, Sybil. *Inside Bellevue*. New York: Mason/Charter, 1976.

Leek, Sybil. *Telepathy: The "Respectable" Phenomenon*. New York: Macmillan, 1971.

Lingerman, Hal. *The Healing Energies of Music*. Wheaton, IL: Theosophical Publishing House, 1995.

MacLean, Dorothy. *To Hear the Angels Sing: An Odyssey of Co-creation with the Devic Kingdom*. Hudson, NY: Lindisfarne, 1994.

Maharishi Mahesh Yogi. *Science of Being and the Art of Living: Transcendental Meditation*. New York: Plume, 2001.

Massey, Gerald. *The Natural Genesis*. Baltimore: Black Classic, 1998.

McLuhan, Marshall, and Quentin Fiore. *The Medium Is the Message*. New York: Random House, 1967.

Merleau-Ponty, Maurice. *Phenomenology of Perception*. Translated by Colin Smith. London: Rutledge & Kegan, 1962.

Nagy, Andras M. *The Secrets of Pythagoras*. Charleston, SC: CreateSpace, 2007.

Narby, Jeremy. *Intelligence in Nature: An Inquiry into Knowledge*. New York: Jeremy Tarcher, 2005.

Newton, Michael. *Journey of Souls*. St. Paul, MN: Llewellyn, 1999.

Olcott, Henry Steele. *Old Diary Leaves*. Wheaton, IL: Theosophical Publishing House, 1975.

Ostrander, Sheila, Lynn Schroeder, and Ivan T. Sanderson. *Psychic Discoveries behind the Iron Curtain*. New York: Bantam Books, 1971.

Ouspensky, P. D. *In Search of the Miraculous*. Boston: Mariner Books, 2001.

Ouspensky, P. D. *Tertiam Origanum*. Kila, MT: Kessinger, 1998.

Paulson, Genevieve Lewis. *Energy Focused Meditation*. St. Paul, MN: Llewellyn, 1997.

Pierrakos, John. *Core Energetics*. Mendocino, CA: Evolution, 2005.

Plato. *Complete Words by Plato*. Indianapolis, IN: Hackett, 1997.

Puharich, Andeija. *Uri: The Original and Authorized Biography of Uri Geller—the Man Who Baffled Scientists*. London: W. H. Allen, 1974.

Ramsland, Katherine. *Dean Koontz: A Writer's Biography*. New York: Harper Prism, 1997.

Ramsland, Katherine. "Phone Calls from the Dead." *Psychology Today Magazine*, September 27, 2013.

Ritkin, Jeremy. *Entropy: Into the Greenhouse World*. New York: Bantam Books, 1989.

Rogo, D. Scott, and Raymond Bayless. *Phone Calls from the Dead*. Englewood Cliffs, NJ: Prentice-Hall, 1979.

Satchidananda, Sri S. *The Yoga Sutras of Pantanjali*. Buckingham, VA: Integral Yoga Distribution, 1990.

Shelley, Mary, and J. Paul Hunter. *Frankenstein*. New York: W. W. Norton, 2012.

Shroder, Tom. *Old Souls: Compelling Evidence from Children Who Remember Past Lives*. New York: Simon & Schuster, 2001.

Skolimowski. Henryk. *Theatre of the Mind*. Wheaton, IL: Quest Books, 1984.

Smith, Ingram. *Truth Is a Pathless Land: A Journey with Krishnamurti*. Wheaton, IL: Quest Books, 1989.

Smith, Penelope. *Animal Talk: Interspecies Telepathic Communication*. Point Reyes Station, CA: Pegasus, 1996.

Smith, Penelope. *Animals . . . Our Return to Wholeness*. Point Reyes Station, CA: Pegasus, 1993.

Steiger, Brad. *One with the Light: Authentic Near-Death Experience That Changed Lives and Revealed the Beyond*. New York: Signet Books, 1994.

Steiger, Brad. *Words from the Source*. Englewood Cliffs, NJ: Prentice- Hall, 1975.

Stevenson, Ian. *Children Who Remember Previous Lives*. Jefferson, NC: McFarland, 2000.

Stone, Robert B. *The Secret Life of Your Cells*. Atglen, PA: Schiffer, 1997.

Thompkins, Peter, and Christopher Bird. *The Secret Life of Plants*. New York: Harper & Row, 1989.

Thompson, Peter, and Christopher Bird. *Secrets of the Soil*. Anchorage, AK: Earthpulse, 1998.

Vance, Bruce A. *Dreamscape: Voyage in an Alternate Reality*. Wheaton, IL: Quest Books, 1995.

Vance, Bruce A. *Mindscape: Exploring the Reality of Thought Forms*. Wheaton, IL: Quest Books, 1995.

Webster, Richard. *Aura Reading for Beginners*. St. Paul, MN: Llewellyn, 1998.

Weschcke, Carl, and Joe Slate. *Self-Empowerment and the Subconscious*. Woodbury, MN: Llewellyn, 2018.

Wood, Ernest. *The Seven Rays*. Wheaton, IL: Theosophical Publishing House, 1972.

INDEX